Reasoning From Beyond
The Tombs

Reasoning From Beyond The Tombs

Ngô Tôn-Long

iUniverse, Inc.
New York   Bloomington

Reasoning from beyond the tombs

Copyright © 2010 by Ngô Tôn-Long

iUniverse books may be ordered through booksellers or by contacting:

iUniverse
1663 Liberty Drive
Bloomington, IN 47403
www.iuniverse.com
1-800-Authors (1-800-288-4677)

Because of the dynamic nature of the Internet, any Web addresses or links contained in this book may have changed since publication and may no longer be valid.

ISBN: 978-1-4401-8882-4 (sc)
ISBN: 978-1-4401-8883-1 (ebk)

Printed in the United States of America

iUniverse rev. date: 1/13/2010

NGÔ TÔN-LONG
1940–1975
Graduated from the National Institute of Pedagogy, Saigon 1956–1959
And the Faculty of Pedagogy, Dalat 1960–1963
Teacher of Mathematics and Philosophy at high-schools, 1959–1975
Lecturer on Philosophy and Pedagogy at Dalat University, 1968–1975

יהוה

The burden of your will is heavy of your will is heavy"

Upon me

A tiny piece of dust

Off the ground

These thirty five years now

Off the ground in that enclosed large graveyard called paradise red or socialist for the eleven years 1975–1986, the dust had evolved into a piece of 'rock hewn not by men'. Then the rock has been made harder and harder—enough not only to stand the wars of 1976, 1979 … 1989 all over that miserable peninsula, a much larger graveyard torn by the rising Chinese and the falling Soviets both self-called international socialists; but also to take up the Reasoning Challenge for a world without Religious Wars—the Ancient World of the Hebrew Sojourners that has been lost ever since Moses the Israelite from Egypt made out 'in his own image and according to his own likeness' A Man Of War:

"The LORD is a man of war, LORD is his name"

Then, sang Moses and the Children of Israel this song unto
YHVH and the Children of Israel this song unto YHVH"

I will sing unto YHVH
For he has triumphed gloriously
The horse and its rider
He has thrown into the sea
YHVH is my strength and song is my strength and song"
And he has become my salvation
He is my God and I will prepare him a habitation and I will
prepare him a habitation"
My father's God and I will exalt him and I will exalt him"
The LORD is a Man of War
LORD is his Name

(Exodus, Chapter XV, Verses 1–3)

Contents

Prologue

There have been wars and wars, among humans ever since the beginning as well as among gods even before that beginning. Both are not religious wars in the sense used here—humans create gods and/or goddesses in order to make wars in their name(s), most if not all the times in the common honorific title God, likely a self-same one, at all warring sides.

Over four hundred years prior to Moses, in Mesopotamia, his forefather Abram had won over the warring kings north of Damascus with some hundreds of his servants, not taking anything 'even a thread or a sandal strap'—let alone his adversaries' wives and children, cities and houses, wealth and possession. Even the piece of land called 'Cave of Machpelah at the end of a field' Abraham would pay four hundred shekels of silver, currency of the merchants, for the burial place of the *Hebrew sojourners* from Mesopotamia. No gods were involving therein.

But in Canaan, Abraham's heir-son Isaac, born to him at his 100th year of age, caused troubles to the 14-year older heir-presumptive Ishmael. The half-brother's descendants have been warring against one another generation after generation <u>all over the millennia up until nowadays</u>. And worse things came by the contention between Isaac's twin-sons over the birthright, blessing, and heir-ship—of which Jacob was the *usurper and winner*. Then the worst of things did come after Jacob was renamed *Isra-el* because of his 'struggle with God' and with men, pre-vailing both; Or *Is-ra-el* for his being the 'man who sees God' and lives; Let alone the clearly apologetic distortion: Israel wrestled *for God against men* and prevailed *them*. Two out of Israel's twelve sons, Simeon and Levi, did nothing either for God or for Israel when they 'deceitfully killed King Hamor and his son, Prince Shechem, massacred all males of Shechem city, took captive all their wives and children, and plun-dered all their wealth in the field and in the city and in the houses'. <u>Ages later</u>, without any sort of the so-called Dinah cause or excuse, many such invading and terminating campaigns would be conducted allegedly *Under God* or *At Commandments* by the Israelites, actually under Moses and Aaron from

Egypt, then under Joshua toward and into the land Canaan—both phases of their Religious War were 'After the Ark of *Covenant*', a Sacred Movable Container, housing explicitly the *Ten Com-mandments* on the two tablets of stone and implicitly the *"Man of War"*.

There had never been any such things before—ever since 'the beginning' throughout the whole lot of Patriarchs as recorded from Adam the first Human to Abram the first Hebrew. Eons prior to Abram and the Hebrews, the Creator namely YHVH had been called on, even Abram was told by YHVH to 'get out of birth-place, from relatives and father's house'. Then, over four hundred years after Abram, the self-same God 'appeared to Moses in a bush burning yet not consuming, and revealed to Moses *The Name YHVH for the first time*'—actually not *The Name* but the meaning *Eh Yeh asher Eh Yeh*, of same Hebrew root, was recorded first by Moses together with his innovation *Man of War*. The English rendering 'I Am who I Am' is much more obscure than the original Hebrew, likewise is the differentiation of Jesus from Jos-hua—one and the same Hebrewיהושע —both Latinised names are meaning: YHVH saves saves" , YHVH will save, or YHVH be saviour. None others, but YHVH, can save, nor Joshua neither Jesus; let alone Moses the god-man or demi-god of the Egyptian style—whose Religion, called Mosaic after himself or Israelite after his subjects, proved itself incapable to maintain their Monarchy, Kingdom(s), and Temples.

That was because, after having executed Moses' inhumane measures to an overall triumph against almost all peoples of the land Canaan, the Israelites *resumed* their perennial 'Struggle with God': Doing evil in his sight, serving gods of the land, everyone doing what was *right in one's own eyes*. As a whole, Israel prevailed over God and his prophet Samuel, asking for a king to become *Like all the nations*, that is, rejecting God his Rulership: The *Israelite God* had been '*dead* to the Israelites' so long before Friedrich Nietzsche (1844–1900) the most famous non-Jewish Jew proclaimed 'that *death* to the Jews' in the ending of the 19th century CE. However, by the end of the so-called Hebrew Prophecy, there was an anonymous prophet *still* taking up Moses' viewpoint, laws, and strategies. *"Was Esau not Jacob's brother? Yet I loved Jacob and hated Esau"*—as if YHVH were a human of favou-ritism and caprices, hatred and wars, promises and threats, that is, all sorts of religious facilities not compatible with the Creator who de-clares, "I am YHVH, I do not change", in that book named by the Hebrew term for 'my messenger' *mal-aki*. YHVH does not change, humans used to change themselves and do change YHVH as well: They made their God into Man, housed their Creator inside Container of sorts, and suppressed at will The Name—even substituted it by the title *Adonai* meaning 'Lord', hence 'namings': LORD, Jahve, and so on.

The First Jerusalem Temple, c. 960–586 BCE, King Solomon built not to house The God, only dedicated to The Name. But that Second one, c. 486 BCE–70 CE, was housing both God and Name in its Holy of Holies till the Great Destruction by the Romans—a generation after Jesus. This Jesus, the Jew of Nazareth, came to the Hellenised Jews in Judea then under Roman rulership, preaching them their FATHER's Sovereign Rulership at hand, *"Neither here nor there but within you"*. Most of them heard of a 'kingdom in heaven' but did not see the Heavenly Kingship. Few of them saw a kingship in Jesus, being at their hand, for their forefathers' kingdom(s) lost so long ago—that they would take Jesus by force in order to make out a 'lord', another 'man of war' in the Moses-style, fighting for them and restoring them their kingdom.

Jesus escaped them to his FATHER (alone) he defined <u>Spirit, not Man</u> (that is, of dust), as he was teaching <u>Love, neither Hatred nor War</u>. Going on the way of all humans, he passed away and was made 'Lord and Saviour'—despite his Hebrew name שוהי□ meaning: הוהי be Saviour. This repetition is needed because the scripts are preserved up to this very day but pronunciations and meanings were either lost along the way of exiles and deportations, or distorted due to integrations and assimilations. Another convention differentiating Lord (Jesus) from LORD (YHVH) was made in order that Jesus can save: *A man* can 'save his people from their sins' in the stead of *The Spirit*.

The ancient Joshua could not save because *only Jesus the name* was made 'above all names, unique to call on for *the* salvation, at which should bow every knee of those *in heaven* and *on earth* and *under earth*. The Name YHVH *was* substituted, suppressed, and *forbidden* in order that 'the Alpha and the Omega, the Beginning and the End, the First and the Last, the Root and the Offspring of King David (that is Jesus) *is coming quickly ... surely quickly*, for the time is at hand'—as foretold almost two millennia ago.

The pronunciation and meaning of The Name were lost, the 586-BCE Destruction and Exile by the Babylonians caused it all. Out of Exile-and-Diaspora emerged the 'Second Moses' Ezra; under the Persian rule and auspices he established his *Judaism*—Religion by, of, and for *Jews*; with his newly instituted system of *Synagogues* in the stead of the First Temple, with Cyrus the Persian king made into an An-ointed or Christ, and, at completion of the Second Temple, a century later, with its new politico-religious *Sanhedrin*. All and altogether were to be desecrated by the Syrians, then destroyed by the Romans.

By the 70-CE Destruction, and ultimately by the 135-CE Deportation and Great Diaspora, The Name had been *forbidden to be pronounced outside the Holy of Holies for over half a millennium.* Ever since, Jews and Judaism have become an Inseparable One, so that Jesus of Nazareth *was* a Jew whereas many a *Christ* is not. There are as many *Christs* as *Christian-isms*—Religions by, of, and for Christians; altogether covered under the uttermost convenient term *Christianity*; being factually literal deri-vatives from Judaism as their Sacred Texts 'borrow' one form or an-other of the Hebrew Scripture. The borrowings proceed throughby distorted translations and interpretations, deformed rearrangements and interpolations—let alone the outright innovative additions upon which a new Holy Book was created by dozen of First Christians, among whom Saul of Tarsus being the Foremost of all: Saint Paul is to be accounted for the making up *Christ The Saviour* out of Jesus the Jew, that is, the non-Jewish (ethnically) non-Judaic (religiously) *Christ-Jesus*. *Saul* made himself first non-Judaic, then became *Paolos* with his Greek *Christos*, and was finally canonised as *Paulus* together with the Latin *Christus*. The First Christianism of his had been Hellenised and Roma-nised well before it seemed to Christianise the Roman Emperor and Empire in *Anno Domini 312*. There had been no such thing called Chri-stianisation prior to AD 425 when the *Roman Catholicism* was set up—afterward, so, the thing should rather be Catholicisation, not Christian-isation. However, during the period 135–425 CE, outside the Roman *Aelia Capitolina* and *Syria Palaestina*, that First Christianism did get the upper hand over Judaism and against all heterodoxies of sort.

Some small-scale Moses-style Religious Wars did resume and, ever since AD 312, have been conducted under this *heavenly sign*, at that *godly commandment*, on one or another of the *religious pretexts*—even of the actual *religiously believed pretexts* on humanity, history, civilisation, and so on; the *anti-terrorism*, in particular, included as being conducted with *all sorts of terrors*. Nowadays the world powers are making large-scale in-vading and exterminating wars against one another, still on religious and/or religiously believed pretexts perennial and universal, for their ephemeral desires and material profits. From *Beyond The Tombs* 2005–2007, and upon the 2009 Vietnamese text of *Posthumous Miscellany* 1975–2010, this *Reasoning* is to clarify the millennia-old cloudy under-standing on The Name YHVH—a sort of mission impossible ***if not given*** the accumulated efforts already made by non-Jewish Jews whose dated reasonable contributions are briefly acknowledged hereafter.

- The Mosaic Law (*Torah*) contained ideas inspired, but not written, by God—partly, but not wholly, by Moses (1800s);

- Different human writers and transmitters (*Neviim*) absorbed, adapted, combined previous materials, written but mostly oral, into The Scripture (*Tanakh*) (1920s);) absorbed, adapted, combined previous materials, written but mostly oral, into The Scripture (*Tanakh*) (1920s);"
- Anonymous talented writers edited, redacted, interpolated, and even inserted into, everyone of all Books (*Scrolls*) with their own works—The Writings (*Kethuvim*) in particular (1950s);) with their own works—The Writings (*Kethuvim*) in particular (1950s);"
- So much so that, after all, Judaism is believed as an 'evolving religious *Civilisation*'—not a Religion with the *Personal Deity* who *chose the People*, but merely a *Culture and Identity* with adherence to *Humanistic Values* (1960s).

Not in line with the latter, Humanistic Judaism, however, this *Reasoning* is on Spirituality, the Ancient Hebrews' Spirituality with their Personal YHVH, the very Creator הוהי self-existing (creating and not created):

- Discovered <u>as never been ever taught of before</u>—Part I
- Changed into a <u>Man of War</u> by the man of Religious War—P. II—P. II"
- Deported, Exiled, and <u>Globalised</u> by the 'Second Moses'—P. III'—P. III"
- Replaced by many a <u>Saviour from Sins</u>—Part IV *from Sins*—Part IV"

Spirituality is understood here quite differently from Religion. The faith in YHVH might well be religious, yet not religious enough to originate a religion of the sort so established as to be called Monotheism. Other gods the Ancient Hebrews had *not* denied, very many were implicitly *ac-knowledged*, even some explicitly *regarded*. The Hebraic 'henotheism and monolatry' cannot be classified either as monotheism or as polytheism: The Hebrews *from the other side of the river* were '<u>called to testify to YHVH</u>' amidst the polytheistic world of the Ancient Near-East—not to exter-minate its gods, neither to destroy it nor to *convert and save* it, the pre-Abrahamic world <u>without religions monotheistic</u>, that is, <u>without wars religious.</u>

This is irreligious, *not anti-religious*, a study consulting mainly the *Hebrew –English* scriptural volumes listed as follows (no bibliography available)
- *The NIV Triglot Old Testament*, 1981, Zondervan Pub. USA, 1981, Zondervan Pub. USA"

- *The Holy Scriptures of the Old Testament*, 1997, British & Foreign Bible Society Pub. UK
- *The Jerusalem Bible*, 2000, Koren–Jerusalem, Pub. Israel
- *The Holy Scriptures*, 2003, Sinai–Tel Aviv, Pub. Israel

An introductory note is due to the 1911-old *first* Vietnamese version of the *Holy Bible containing the Old Testament and the New Testament*, published by the Christian Missionary Association for the Vietnamese Evangelical Church, last reissued *verbatim* in 1985 by the United Bible Societies, and particularly *deprived of the* <u>unintentionally inspiring particular</u> by the 2002-new *New Translation*—Arms of Hope, Pub. Singapore.

The 1911 Vietnamese *New Testament of OUR LORD JESUS CHRIST* had <u>no SAVIOUR in the title on the title-page</u> and was paginated from -1- to -326- (the two, last and blank, pages were not paginated)—separately from the *Old Testament* (from page -1-: *The First Book of Moses called Genesis*; to page -1070-: *The Book of Malachi*, Chapter 4, The Great Day of Jehovah). There are rooms there for YHVH, The Creator as named at *Genesis 2:4*, to be <u>SAVIOUR</u> in the separate 328-page *Book*.

Not so with the 2002 Vietnamese *New Translation* which has *The Old Testament*, pp. 1–1106, followed by *The New Testament*, pp. 1107–1448, directly and without any epithets at all for both title-pages. How-ever *Testament* has been rendered still appropriately by the Vietnamese term accurately corresponding to the Hebrew <u>brit—covenant, contract;</u> not evidence, neither witness, <u>nor will</u>. There are *no testaments* either in the Tanakh or in the Gospel(s): *The Covenant(s)* there used to be Hellenised into <u>Diatheke—Covenant</u>, *Will*; hence *New Testament* then *Old Testament*.

And another Vietnamese, a phrase, *having also persisted* ever since the first version, through the second translation, up until nowadays, is actually <u>inspiring</u>—now intentionally because clearly mistranslated (with add-ins), from the Hebrew *'Eh Yeh'* meaning *'I Am'* to '<u>Self-Existing and Ever-Existing</u>', in both Vietnamese sentences for *Exodus 3:14* (<u>p. 66</u>)

- *I am* (that/what/who *I am*) the *Self-Existing and Ever-Existing*;
- Tell the Children of Israel that (*I Am*) the *Self-Existing and Ever-Existing* has sent you to them—YHVH was speaking to Moses. that (*I Am*) the *Self-Existing and Ever-Existing* has sent you to them—YHVH was speaking to Moses."

Traditionally familiar add-ins for '<u>Eh Yeh asher Eh Yeh</u>' and henceforth for <u>The Name YHVH</u> are summarised as an introduction to Part I:' and henceforth for <u>The Name YHVH</u> are summarised as an introduction to Part I:"

- I am who I am; *(there's nothing to do with you)*
- I will be what I will be; *(there's nothing for you to do)*
- I am *The One* that causes/ will cause *everything* to be/ exist;
- I am *The One* that causes/ will cause *my covenant/ plans/ promises* to be/ become *fulfilled/ come true.*

Peculiarly seemed the 1911-Vietnamese rendering to have come in line with the 2000-Koren's in their *Jerusalem Bible—The Holy Scriptures* (<u>p. 65</u>)

The Creator

○ ○

YHVH::"

"I will ever be what I now am"

> *Exodus 3:14—Koren Pub. 2000 3:14—Koren Pub. 2000"*

These are the geneses of skies and earth when created in the day YHVH made it

> *Genesis 2: 4*

The Creation

The Hebrew 'toledoth' used to be translated literally into generations, or literary into histories then history. No geneses of whatever things at wherever places can be stated scientifically without an axiom, mentally without a belief, or religiously without a faith. The Hebrew spirituality meant something in-between intellectual and religious; Abram of Ur in Mesopotamia was called to believe in and walk after YHVH from the side of the river there—leaving behind him that world *of the gods on high* and, as well, *of their worshippers on earth*; his father, relatives, and compa-triots included. *Enuma Elish* (When on High) is the Mesopotamian story on the creation of everything, gods and their universe, the earth and humans, ...The wisdom-god Ea was recorded on a clay-tablet as maker of other gods 'out of clay'; the sea-god Apsu once wanted to de-stroy all 'bothering gods' but his wife, the sea-goddess Tiamat, did not, and as Ea heading the gods to kill her husband she revolted together with the rebellious god Kingu; 'Ea and his gods' then made out the king-god Marduk to slay Tiamat—making the universe 'out of her corpse'; Marduk also slew Kingu—forming a man 'out of his blood'.

The English 'creation' and 'to create' used to be used indiffer-ently whether or not the creature is out of stuff/ material/ ... whereas, in Hebrew, YHVH The Creator created (*bara*) out of nothing (*ex nihilo*) skies and earth and humans, but made (*asa*)/ formed (*yasar*) from initial (*ex initio*) male and female, human as well as animal—explicitly an *adam* out of dust (*efer*) taken from the ground (*adamah*), *dam* meaning blood is the root of both *adamah* and *adam*. The scriptural 'adam' was meaning first humankind as a whole, and second a human/ an individual, before becoming the personal name of the first man Adam. The earliest to be known statement quite materialist is at Genesis 2:7, "YHVH formed an *adam* from the dust taken out of the ground". Materialistically another *adam* might have been (re)created in a 1953-laboratory, from a mixture of methane, ammonia, hydrogen, and water—were Stanley Miller then able to get those 'miraculous historical accumulations' of recipes for, of the conditions of, the so-called 'Life at its Origin'. Scientific researches have since discovered amino acids the building blocks of proteins, nu-cleic acids the basis for protein synthesis and genetic transmission, ri-bonucleic acids the single-strand self-reproducing molecules, and some things 'simpler-than yet dissimilar-from' those latter ...at Origin of Life.

Dust of the ground

Adamah, the ground, is so the stated whereabout life on earth had once originated from. How? Nobody knows, it is not stated, and scientists have not known as yet—otherwise they could have made out some sort of artificial life wherefrom, 'made out' being quite far from 'created', so is 'out of *dust*' from 'out of IVF-*ovum* or DNA-*clone*'. And when? None of the proposed dates can be ascertained, six to twelve thousand years ago, or some billions of years before the present (BP)!

Taking *dust* for granted as eternal, materialistic evolutionists had come up with the so-called *a-bio-genesis*, a theory positing *matter* at the beginning 10–20 billion years BP. Actually that *dust* cannot be eternal, a tiny *speck of vacuum* is then postulated in order that there *be* the so-called 'Primordial Physical Vacuum *Energy*—this very one is verily eternal, by itself capable to convert itself into one or another *form*: It caused a 'Big Bang' at c. 15 billion year BP. Within 10-43second, completed were the beginning of time and the formation of space-time as a whole in the 4-dimension structure. By 10-40second the universe had been driven to an enormous size by repulsive gravity, the cosmic inflation then originated the cosmic expansion that has since been working up until nowadays.

About 10-4second, the Primordial Energy converted itself into thermal radiation, creating light-particles (quanta/photons) and matter-particles as well as anti-particles. Meanwhile the repulsive gravity be-came attractive, remaining such familiar to this day as the background radiation energy and the cosmic dark matter dominating the universe as well as its mass. So, within *one second* all things were settled: time, space, light, matter, quantum fluctuation, radiation energy, quarks, electrons, baryonic and normal matters, proton, neutrons, neutrinos, positrons ...

About 13 billion year BP nuclei of light elements, e. g. helium, was created and nuclei of hydrogen recombined by 12.5 billion year BP —afterwards began the formation of galaxies of stars and quasars, of this solar system including this earth, completed by 4.5 billion year BP ready for the emergence of organic molecules, out of an atmosphere containing hydrogen, methane, ammonia, and vapor of water, under sunlight or lightning or volcanic heat: Chemical reactions did it all there —fortunately *there had been no oxygen yet*. Hundreds of millions of years later, the <u>organic molecules</u> *increased and concentrated in the oceans* enough enormously to give birth to <u>living organisms</u> that would keep on evol-ving into <u>life</u>: All and altogether, everything from *dust* to *life* did emerge out of that so-called 'marine solution' or 'Primordial Soup'.

> *YHVH formed an <u>adam</u> from the dust taken out of <u>adamah</u>, and breathed into his nostrils the <u>neshamah ... of life</u>: <u>adam became living</u> a <u>nephesh</u>.*
>
> —*Genesis 2: 7*

> *... All flesh in which is the <u>ruah of life</u> ... shall die*
>
> —*Genesis 6: 17*

... All in whose nostrils was the <u>neshamah-ruah of life</u> died

—*Genesis 7: 22*

The Spirit

The Hebrew 'nephesh' is for an individual/ a being, actually living as a whole, inseparably flesh and blood and breath and so on <u>bodily</u>—*fish, bird, cattle, beast, humans <u>male and female</u>*. This is to point out that the three above quotes, 'neshamah' and 'ruah' and 'neshamah-ruah' of 'nephesh', are meaning something not bodily, maybe never noted as up to Jesus (Yeshuah) the Jew of Nazareth who came defining *<u>The Spirit</u> to be worsh-ipped <u>in spirit and in truth</u>*—wherein 'YHVH The Spirit' bestowed '*spirit of life*' upon the first 'adam' named Adam so that Adam became '*spiritly li-ving*', that is, living in spirit (and in truth, as *Son of The Spirit*)

YHVH The Spirit is nowhere demonstrated in the Scriptures, cannot be either visualised or fathomed. 'To believe or not to believe, that is the question'. On the other hand The Spirit has got no body nor image neither likeness—his creatures have, so had the aforementioned Mesopotamian gods (Ea, … Marduk) as well as the Ugaritic and Cana-anite gods to be mentioned only El the chief-god and his wife Asherah the goddess. This is to point out sort of evolution from Ea through El to the Hebrew 'eloah'/ a god and 'elohim'/ gods—hence 'In the begin-ning *Elohim* created heavens and earth … In *Elohim's own image* humans male and female were created'. Genesis 1: 1, 27.

Moreover, Genesis 5: 1, 3 explicitly stated the *likeness of Elohim* <u>only in Adam</u>: Adam begot a son 'in his own likeness, after his image'. Nothing to do with The Spirit, <u>then and ever afterwards</u>. A witness has recently witnessed like this: I was born in my father's image and after my father's likeness; he in his father's and after his father's; ...so I am in God's image and after God's likeness—completely ignoring the whole lot of often-time down-grading and quite rarely up-grading evolutions throughout the thousands if not billions of years past. Let alone the problems regarding the sort of God, or gods, one actually is referring to. This is to point out that humans used to create gods and goddesses in their own image, according to their own likeness—for their own uses. Even YHVH The Spirit was made into a '<u>Man Of War</u>' for the Israelites' exterminating conquest all over the peoples and lands of Canaan—Chapter 2. On the contrary, Jesus the man was transfigured into a <u>God</u> (<u>The Son</u>) and assigned the job of a <u>Lord Saviour</u>—Ch.4.

*"Of every tree in the garden, you may **freely** eat*
*But of the tree '**knowledge of good and evil**' you shall not*
*For **in** the day you eat of it you shall **surely die**."*

Genesis 2: 16–17

The Covenant

Above quoted is a covenant/contract, not commandment. Humans are absolutely free to accept and observe it or not. The Covenant proposed by The Spirit is completely spiritual, not material, and definitely eternal, not eventual. YHVH did not command Adam *not* to eat a so-called *forbidden fruit.* Given the spirit of life to live spiritually (in the spirit/*presence* of YHVH), Adam was told, *"If you <u>become like YHVH</u> to <u>know/determine what is good</u> and <u>what is evil</u>, then you are <u>out of the spirit of YHVH.</u>"*

Misleading are the renderings/implications: (to) Command, the Life (bodily everlasting), (to) Die (bodily) In The (thousand-year) Day, the (forbidden) Knowledge/Understanding (general and scientific)—henceforth Original Sin, Lost Paradise, Salvation Plan(s), and so on up to this very scholarly verbatim exegesis "As distinct from beasts, hu-mans are *intelligent* because, against the *command* of God, they obtained and ate *magic fruit* from the *Tree of Knowledge*, thus gaining *Knowledge* that up to that time had been a *monopoly of divinity*, not intended for humans. The antonyms 'good and evil' mean *everything* here, and humans share with God his *divine prerogative, the faculty of Universal Knowledge.* This is not the 'Fall of Man' but rather the *Rise of Man Halfway to Divinity*: Man was checked from obtaining *Immortality.*"

Bodily there is no such thing called immortality, 'dust of the ground' is to 'return as dust *to the ground*' sooner or later. The perennial illusions of an everlasting life, sorts of resurrection and life-after-death did have come from *the other magic fruit*—from the 'Tree of Life' *lost yet soon and very soon coming down out ot heaven.* The asymmetric antonyms 'Life' and 'Knowledge-of-Good-and-Evil' *there*, neither mean 'every-thing'—rather two *opposite choices*: Obedience to the Creator and Living in the Spirit, or Disobedience and '*Going out from the Presence of YHVH.* Human used to rise oneself all the way up to sorts of divinity, deciding what is good and what is evil *for everyone else*, 'doing what is right *in one's own eyes*', judging others according to one's own criteria/ determination if not prejudices/ imagination.

Adam chose *his woman Eve* instead of *his creator YHVH*, Eve the woman chose a thing *she deemed good* for food and *pleasant* to (her) eyes and *desirable* to make (her) wise—sorts of determinative disobedience. chose *his woman Eve* instead of *his creator YHVH*, Eve the woman chose a thing *she deemed good* for food and *pleasant* to (her) eyes and *desirable* to make (her) wise—sorts of determinative disobedience."

> *"You shall eat bread in the sweat of your face* **till you return to the ground**
>
> *… Dust you are,* **to dust** *you are* **to return.** *"*

Genesis 3: 19

The spiritual death

Immediately at disobedience there is the spiritual death. No needs to invent a literary thousand-year *day*. 'Return to dust' is the very sentence —humans *without the spirit* always are *dust*. Return to the ground, *bodily die*, there, is no sentence—'till you die bodily' clearly is a circumstancial clause. YHVH The Spirit clearly did not sentence Adam and Eve to die bodily *on* the day or *within* a thousand year: They were clothed then sent *out of his presence* for 'all the days' of their life.

Their son Cain once got 'very angry' because his offering was not accepted, YHVH then covenanted, "*If* you do well, will you not be accepted? *And if* you do not do well, *sin lies at the door—its desire is for you, you should rule over it.*" Cain would <u>not</u>. He was driven <u>*off the presence of YHVH*</u>, not killed but even granted a mark set to protect him from be-ing killed. This is to point out the <u>*unique*</u> '*sin against YHVH*', <u>*disobedience*</u> —to which the sentence is verily the spiritual death.

You have got no faith-in-YHVH at all. No problems whatever for you to go <u>completely and absolutely free</u> 'the way of all the earth'. And no worry whenever some believers say you <u>*are dead to YHVH*</u> because they actually mean YHVH <u>*was already dead to you*</u>, knowing it or not. You are not burdened with the '*neshamah-ruah* of life' whereas they were: Their forefathers in those not so good old days, called *sons of God*, 'saw the beautiful *daughters of humans*, chose whom they liked to be their *wives*, begot by them *giants on earth—mighty ones of renown*, and *caused* whereby the great wickedness all over the earth. YHVH then decided, "My *Ruah* shall not abide in *adam* forever for *adam* is indeed *flesh*."—6:3

Genesis 6:17 states, 'all *flesh* in which is the *ruah* of life ... shall die'. Then 7:22 concludes 'All in whose nostrils *was neshamah-ruah* of life *died*'. This is to point out that the flesh of <u>all sons of God</u> then on earth was destroyed—meanwhile the children of *humans*, daughters and sons, being not targetted, might well have perished alongside, also flesh indeed, all and altogether. On the other hand, the 'spirit of life' or the 'breath of spirit of life' deprived of *all flesh* could no longer do either evil or good: Driven <u>out of flesh</u> and <u>having done evil</u>, the 'spirits' (spiritly beings or spirit-creatures) could *never return to their Creator—YHVH The Spirit (RUAH)*, they began to 'hover all over the earth, go to-and-fro and walk back-and-forth on it', as 'fugitives and vagabonds' there.

The spiritly creatures

Spirit- or spiritly denotes something *unknown and unknowable*, unfathomable at best to believers, *given from YHVH The Spirit* upon human (of flesh-and-blood-and-so-on as an inseparable whole). Unbelievers have got their full rights to deny both Spirit and spirit-beings: Atheists how-ever do believe their atheisms, not one but many an –ism of sort. Like-wise, infidels used to recognise sort of God-Creator but refuse the gift of loving-and-caring Spirit: Deists maintain their Creator too transcen-dent to love and care for them. Theistic believers used on the contrary to use their God for even their bodily aspiration and daily needs, at the uttermost are the so-called immortality if still living, and resurrection if going to die. The Spirit has got nothing to do with all such –isms, ever since 'Adam begot a son *in his own likeness after his image*'—no connective in Hebrew for the English 'and' there.

On the other hand, YHVH <u>*never*</u> gets any <u>*image*</u> and had once for all decided <u>*not*</u> to let part and parcel of <u>*his spirit abide forever in the flesh*</u> of any son of God—messenger and prophet of earlier times, priest and king later on. Immediately whenever a son of this sort sinned against YHVH he died <u>spiritly</u>—until he repented and was resurrected <u>spiritly</u>. It had been not so before The Flood: The sons of God then sinned greatly and were given years to repent, but they would *not to* and their flesh was destroyed definitely—whenceforth the *spirit-creatures*: spirit of evil, spirit of lie, and so on. YHVH did not create them, *the evil spirits per se*, as usually misunderstood; neither did YHVH *the hosts of good spirits* called angels and archangels and things of that heaven-servicing *army*, as traditionally imagined.

Nor did YHVH make *humankind* <u>in order that they worship and serve</u> a *kingdom of heaven*—with their praises and offerings and sacrifices *from the surface of this earth*, as religiously ordained in all sorts of *earthly religions*. In the Hebrew Scriptures, there is not a 'kingdom of heaven', any ways, but instead *the kingship* or *rulership—<u>spiritly over good and evil</u>*. A reasoning like this, "There is no use <u>being god</u> in heaven(s) unless there are humans <u>worshipping and providing</u> from earth", may fit very well any gods of an earthy pantheon; not *The Spirit-and-Creator* unseen and unseeable, unknown and unknowable. This is to point out that YHVH *be not* of the sorts of God (*El*) and/or gods (*elohim*)—until *being made so*

- Namely: Yahweh, Jehovah, Jahve, ...,
- Descriptively: Volcanic God, Cruel Ogre, Evil Monster, ...,
- First and foremost: 'Man-Of-War'.

2

A Man Of War

Moses from Egypt

Moses was born Egyptian, maybe at Heliopolis, previously On, north-eastern of the Egyptian Delta, in a region called Goshen, to Amram and Jochebed of the tribe Levi in the 13th century BCE. His Egyptian name *Mose* meant simply 'son' or 'is born'—prefixed by names of gods in Egyptian theophorous kings, Pharaohs, such as *Ahmose* (son of god *Ah*, god *Ah* is born human), *Thutmose* or *Tuthmose*, etc. Pharaohs were gods born human, sons of gods, demi-gods to become gods again at death. A modern author identifies Moses with an Egyptian name *Tuth-mosis* 'a shadowy figure, actually the true heir to the throne' of Amon-hotep III, 'mysteriously disappeared from the record a few years before the reign of Amonhotep IV'—this very latter made himself *Akhen-Aton* that is, Akhenaton or Akhenaten, King Amonhotep III's true son.

Akhenaton's supposedly adopted older brother *Tuth-Mose* was Moses, a royal *prince* fallen from favour and *exiled*, being not the king's true son. This very *Tuthmose* abandoned the old Egyptian gods, drop-ped the god-element *Tuth*, and became *Mose* that is *Moshe* in Hebrew or *Mosis* in the Greek translation Septuagint. But according to the original Hebrew Tanakh, Moshe is said to have become *son* of the Pharaoh's daughter who named him so 'because I *drew* him out of the water'—as if an Egyptian princess were knowing that much Hebrew. A reasonable synthesis may well be like this: The Israelite woman, a sister or mother, who saw the princess *draw* the (unnamed) three-month old child from water and who was asked to nurse it, did first name it *Moshe*; as the princess later adopted *the son* and made him *a prince* she named him *Mose*. No need of inventing any names like Tuthmose, nor grounds to suppose Moses being Akhenaton's (adopted) older brother, neither uses of creating an Egyptian Moses in contradiction to the (Israelite) Midian Moses. Sufficient is the Egypto-Israelite Moses of the Scripture.

The twelve-tribe Israelites had by then prospered in male popu-lation from about seventy to well over half a million—the ten genera-tions of theirs successively under slavery, 'groaning because of the Egy-ptian bondage', for those four hundred years. Not included therein were the previous thirty years or so of Joseph's sojourn—as a sold slave, then a misjudged prisoner, till the very acting 'governor over my house, all my people, and all my land' according to the decree of a Pharaoh who said, "Can we find such a one like this, *a man in whom is the Spirit of God*?'. For sure, the Pharaoh being a demi-god did have his own gods; yet there were no problems for Joseph 'serving' the Egy-tians, king and people, but neither gods nor demi-gods.

Joseph the last of all *foreigners and sojourners from the other side of the river* did well testify to the very Creator God—by then unknown to the Egyp-tians, maybe to other peoples too. Afterwards, unfortunately, 'died Jo-seph, all his brothers, and all that generation', then arose over Egypt new kings who did not know either Joseph or Joseph's testimonies: Generations of Israelite slaves, scripturally fourty years in average each from a father's birth to his heir-son's, seemed to have forgotten their God's Name and Covenant—practising merely as a Custom the 'Cir-cumcision Sign of Covenant': Much later, Moses was recorded as First in revealing the Name and ordering the Custom—or were it the case that he himself *wrote* it all?—together with all the *Five Books of Moses* called *Torah* and translated into the Greek *Pentateuch*!

The Mosaic Religion

Anyway, Moses has so long been revered as Liberator of a People and Founder of their Religion as well as their Nation, the Ancient *Israelites'* theocratic monarchy c. 1250–586 BCE, that it really was 'a deed under-taken lightheartedly especially by one belonging to *that* people': To de-ny Moses being an Israelite (Part I: *Moses an Egyptian*), To assert that an 'Egyptian Moses' being a follower of Akhenaton's unique monotheism (Part II: *If Moses was an Egyptian*), And to proclaim the 'Egyptian origin' of the Mosaic Religion—established all over the Israelite People by an-other 'Midian Moses' (Part III: *Moses, His people, and Monotheistic Religion*) —That was Sigmund Freud (1856–1939), another non-Judaic and non-Jewish Jew, *reasoning on the verges of his as well as his people's tombs*, from Germany 1937 to England 1939.

In a sense, regarding the whole Part I and the subject *Circumci-sion* of Part II, S. Freud posited a *controversy* to the Traditional Religions, Mosaic and Judaic. *Israelite* followers of Moses as well as *Jewish* ones of Ezra, almost a millennium later, both maintained 'the usual assump-tion': An Israelite Moshe delivered his compatriots from the Egyptian bondage, established over them the strictest *Monotheism outside Egypt*, and headed them *towards Canaan* their 'land of promise'—circumcision being their *Patriarch Abraham*'s spiritual 'sign-in-the-flesh' of the Cove-nant' consented with *his YHVH God* at his 99th year of age, over half a millennium prior to Moshe.

Set in the mid-19th century BCE, the Covenant was 'everlasting' for *Abraham* and his *descendants after him* through Isaac and Jacob—Ishmael his heir-presumptive, born to him by the *Egyptian* maidservant Hagar, was circumcised 'that very same day', being *thirteen-year old*.

No other origin of the practice is known: From that spiritual sign-in-the-flesh to later religious ritual and traditional rites, female circum-cision or clitoridectomy included, even to present-day hygienic medical operations, it has been widespread and performed differently in times and places—Canaan, Egypt, Ethiopia, Arabia, … Herodotus the Greek historian of the 5th century BCE did not posit back the custom of cir-cumcision *in Egypt* past Abram's time, the 19th century BCE: It has long been practiced there *ever since* and elsewhere in the *Arab territories* by the other *Semites* ever since *Ishmael* their forefather. The psycho-analytic ar-gument for an Egyptian origin of the circumcision is not tenable— meanwhile the reasoning per analogies for that of monotheism not va-lid: *Adonai* and *Aton* are no names, let alone variants of a self-same 'Name of God', the former being a title and the latter a 'sun-rayed-disc' symbol. The Name in Hebrew was Germanised into *Jahve*: '*Jahve was cer-tainly a volcano-god, a bloodthirsty and uncanny demon*'—E. Meyer cited by S. Freud in *Moses and Monotheism*, 1939 Edition, page 48.

The Freudian *Jahve* and *Moses*

But Egypt has no volcanoes and the mountains of the Sinai peninsula have never been volcanic, a 'Midianite Moses', son-in-law of the priest *Jethro*, was then created to be mediator between the Israelites from Egypt and *Jahve the volcano-demon* of 'Sinai-Horeb'—a volcanic mountain at the border of Sinai eastern end and Arabia western end, 'active up to a late period'. *That* Egyptian Moses, trained in Akhenaton's 'school' and forcing his Aton religion on the Israelites, was then killed by the rebellious people, stubborn and unruly toward him, and replaced with *this* Midianite Moses—masterful, hot-tempered, even violent enough to forge out his Mosaic Monotheism, according to Sigmund Freud (Op. cit.). The murder of (the former) Moses the Egyptian was discovered by Ernst Sellin (p. 94); then in his stead (the latter) Moses the Midia-nite, according to Eduard Meyer, unified the Egyptian Israelites and their related tribes nearby Midian into *a new religion worshipping the volcano-god Jahve in the stead of the Aton*—altogether they were ready to conquer Canaan. That is an abridged 'Historical Novel' on

'*Der Mann Moses und die monotheistische Religion*' which <u>initially</u> was written in order to psycho-analytically demonstrate that <u>Religions</u>, from *Egyptian Atonism* to *Israelite Mosaism*, are *Mythic Reproduction of the universal state of infantile helplessness and dependence, Projection of childish wishes for an omnipotent protector and of an immature heteronomy.* Freud's Psychoanalysis was so neither anti-religious nor scientific, maybe a religio-pseudo science if not religion-fiction.

The Egyptian Monotheism

The Egyptian priest and historian Manetho, c. 300 BCE, wrote his *History of Egypt* in Greek figuring <u>*that Mosis*</u> as the rebellious *priest of the Re sun-cult* expelled from Heliopolis and out of the country—together with the lot of lepers and negroes. Sigmund Freud could have taken the no-tion of an <u>*Egyptian Moses*</u> from Manetho without acknowledging that source, made out his Legendary Moses of the Amarna Age there, and created his *irreligious fictitious literature*, not an anti-religious scientific re-search. A modern historian in *A History of the <u>Jews</u>* (1987) found it 'curi-ous that Sigmund Freud, certainly no anti-Semite, based his work on a *fundamental matrix* of anti-Semitism'—the so-called Ur-libel created by Manetho. It certainly is curious that Freud's thesis was so rejected, his speculation being not 'common' at all but, on the contrary, very highly controversial: The Mosaic Religion was derived from the monotheistic religion of Pharaoh Akhenaton (1370–1358 or 1348–1336 BCE).

Re is the name of the Egyptian sun-god, not *Aton*—the 'Aton' being an ancient symbol, not a name, long forgotten under shadows of named gods prior to 1370 (or 1348) BCE when Pharaoh Amonhotep IV officially re-installed it for his <u>*no name, no image, universal, and unique (exclusively)*</u> Deity, renamed himself Akhe<u>naton</u> launching his universal and unique Religion called <u>Aton</u>ism, and moved to his brand-new capi-tal Akhet<u>aton</u> later known as Amarna mid-way from Heliopolis (of the sun-god *Re*, northern Egypt/ Lower Nile) to Thebes (of the storm-god *Amon*, southern Egypt/ Upper Nile). Hence the so-called *Amarna Age* of <u>twelve years</u> accurately, not seventeen as usually spoken of—the two different periods of time, for Akhenaton properly, were set deliberately by 'schools of thought' for their purposes putting *Moses and his Exodus* either immediately or a little bit longer <u>after the Amarna Age</u> (1358 or 1290, 'in the name' of sciences—psychoanalysis or archaeology).

Let alone the other two <u>datings for Exodus prior to Amarna</u> 'in the name' of either *faith-alone (1440)* or *science-fiction (1360)*. The former was to religiously/ traditionally disregard the whole *Monotheistic Amarna* in order that 'the work of Moses can be seen as <u>a total repudiation of everything that</u> <u>*Ancient Egypt* stood for</u>'. And the latter, by another mo-dern author (1998), is to set the Amarna Age as <u>an immediate result of Exodus</u> seen as the *Act of* *God*: Moses performed his Israelite Exodus from Egypt in 1360 BCE, *thus* *influencing* Amonhotep IV to *become Akhe-naton* in 1359 BCE—the Atonism of the *Amarna Age 1359–1347 BCE* was so derived from *this Moses and his* *1360-BCE Exodus*.

Any ways, inside Egypt and before the Exodus there could be **no Mo-** **saic Religion** whatsoever to incite, or influence, or even originate, the Aton-Religion there. Then *after* the Exodus, Moses having established his religion upon the Israelites *at Sinai*, **definitely not** Amonhotep IV ever *would travel* *there* in order to imitate Mosaism in setting up his *Aton-ism* back in and for Egypt. The other way around is actually likely, this is not to submit unto Manetho's and Freud's *stories on the Egyptian Moses and his Israelite* *subjects* quite after the Amarna Age. The Egypto-Israelite 'man of war', an adopted prince educated and trained 'for wars' *at court*, once having *killed* the 'Egyptian beating one of his brethren'—thus ex-pertly taking *laws and* *Law* into his own hands, might verily well be im-pressed by the manners of thought and action of the 'religious revolu-tionary, *earliest known creator* *of a new religion*—breaking with *Egypt's tradi-tional polytheism*'. Professor Erick Hornung (of Egyptology, at Basel Uni-versity) did appropriately call Akhenaton's newly instituted faith *The Re-ligion of Light—Echnaton: Die* *Religion des Lichtes* © 1995; English transla-tion by David Lorton © 1999, Cornell Paperbacks First printing 2001.

This is to point out that '*the Aton*' cannot be identified as 'the Sun' of the *Re* sun-cult. *It* was neither *sun* nor *disc* in the phrase 'sun-***rayed*** disc', no gods were the *handed-rays* emanating wherefrom— *light* might be, according to *The Great Hymn to the Aton*, a prototype of *Psalm 104*. Anybody, celebrity or not, has got one's full right to revere/wor-ship/serve the sun, a disk, and anything of sort *in Ancient Egypt*; but the 'preeminent Egyptologist', even, could not provide either a *god of light* or an *original One*—an *anonymous* *Great One* 'who became himself *millions*' whereas 'there was a naive belief that God had revealed himself as the One to Adam the first man, with the result that monotheism existed from the very beginning, and that polytheism appeared only later as the result of a *break* with God'. (Op. cit., p. 89)

Be it naively believed, *"there was light"*—primordially and *ex nihi-lo* at this *verus dictum*, *"Let there be light"* (Genesis 1:3). The *One* at that be-ginning had been unknown to the *Mosis in Egypt*, was revealed *somehow as* *"Eh Yeh"* (Chapter 1) in the desert of Midian, and would be recor-ded ages later into the 'Five Books of Moses' as *"Elohim"* by another religion-maker called 'Second Moses' (Chapter 3). Because the Mosaic *God* as well as the

Mosaic *Religion* could not be <u>traced</u> actually through-out his allegedly First Book *Genesis*, both are to be searched for else-where—Egypt his country of 'birth and first-forty-year growth', not a Midianite asylum of his 'second-forty-year refuge'.

The Mosaic God

The Angel <u>or</u> The God who appeared to Moses 'in a flame of fire from the midst of a bush', the fire was burning but the bush not consumed, did <u>not</u> appear to be 'the God of Abraham, the God of Isaac, and the God of Jacob' as recorded three-time emphatically—likely by Moses himself: Never before had there been such scenario so miraculous. Most likely, things seem to have happened as follows. Moses, at his fortieth year of (enough grown up) age, once went out to see the Is-raelite slaves at their burdens—having heard of their cry under Egyp-tian bondage/oppression. He saw an Egyptian taskmaster beating a working slave, killed the oppressor and hid his corpse; the following day, he judged over two fighting workers and was denied the judging authority as well as his (adopted prince) royal status. Both execution and judgment <u>of his</u> were known and condemned, Moses fled away as 'Pharaoh sought to kill him'. To Midian, he made fortune, got wife and children, and became famous thanks to his father-in-law—Priest Jethro (*His Excellency*) Reuel of a <u>Midianite religion</u> there.

More likely than God, Moses is it who had *<u>forgotten</u> the 'covenant with Abraham, with Isaac, and with Jacob'* in the process of his forty-year-in -Egypt-plus-another-forty-in-Midian's time—and who, now at the age of eighty, *<u>heard</u> the Children of Israel groaning and crying because of the bondage*, <u>remembered</u> the Covenant and <u>acknowledged</u> the Israelites. This verily mature and clever and experienced hero, then, set out to 'deliver them from the land of bondage and affliction'—making himself ***<u>as God</u>*** to his brother Aaron and his subjects the Israelites, as well as to Pharaoh together with the whole lot of his magicians, exactly and uttermost per-fectly in ***<u>Egyptian style</u>***. This is to point out the Mosaic God in quite different characteristics from the One revealed ages earlier to Abraham and Isaac and Jacob—namely YHVH who did appear and talk to those patriarchs *personally, peacefully, and lovingly*; even *reasoning friendly and humo-rously* with Abraham; or his angel *struggling humanely and reasonably* against Jacob. By the way, the Hebrew *mal-akh* used to be rendered indiffe-rently as *messenger* (from message/*words sent*) or *angel* (from angelos, an-gelus/a *conveyor* of message): YHVH The Creator dealt personally with, directly to, humans his creatures by *word(s) through spirit*—<u>in his like-ness</u>—up to the Deluge. Afterwards humans created sorts of God and gods <u>in their image and according to their likeness</u>:

A 'Man' had replied to Jacob, *"Why is it that you ask about my name?"*; likewise a *'God of Moses'* now warned him, *"I will <u>ever</u> be what I <u>now</u> am. What is it that matters you?"*

Either not recognising the warning or despising it outright, Moses went on with his revolutionary innovations onto his God. Miracle after mira-cle, altogether in the Egyptian magical tradition, the Mosaic God was a-llegedly accounted for the 'ten plagues' against Pharaoh and his Egypt, the *'Red* sea' crossing of 'about six hundred thousand men on foot' not counting children and women and 'a mixed multitude with a great deal of livestock'—as well as the drowning of 'an army of Egyptian horses, chariots, and horsemen and chosen captains, in the midst of the sea'. *So, the people feared the Lord [A Man Of War] and his servant <u>Moses</u> [as <u>God</u>].*

Never before ever had God been made Man, fighting for any people on earth, Hebrew or non-Hebrew: This is verily the first time under Moses and for his Israelite subjects. been made Man, fighting for any people on earth, Hebrew or non-Hebrew: This is verily the first time under Moses and for his Israelite subjects."

Nor any human ever had daringly become God on earth, save the Egyptian pharaohs, to be feared and obeyed and believed in—for-ever and ever: Moses (from Egypt) is second only to Akhenaton.

Neither any peoples ever had been chosen in order to subject and rule all the rest of humankind—the Egyptians under Akhenaton not exempted. Let alone any of all previous Mesopotamian ones. not exempted. Let alone any of all previous Mesopotamian ones."

In the process of time afterwards, during the whole third forty-year pe-riod of Moses' life, wandering round-and-round the desert, the Mosaic God was made, ***among the gods***, into ***a jealous God***. Everything as miraculous as the volcanic appearances was set up for such a God so jealous in order that all the Israelite people ***believe Moses forever***. No wonder therefore, that Sigmund Freud had *mistakenly* identified *that God* with his 'Midianite volcanic demon'—definitely not of the Germanised name he invented out of misunderstanding on both Hebrew and Egyp-tian (Adonai and Aton, for an instance).

The Egyptian *Aton* is not a name, but an ancient symbol visua-lising an invisible no-name God: Pharaoh Amonhotep IV *discovered* the God, *re-instituted* the symbol, and *revolutionised* the Egyptian *system of reli-gions*— radically from polytheistic to *exclusively monotheistic*. Eradicated are the whole lot of traditionally named gods in '*both lands of Egypt*': Amon, Re, Horakhte, Osiris, and so on; even the already combined *Amon-Re, Re-Horakhte*, and the term *gods* on all monuments official as well as ins-criptions private. Meanwhile the Hebrew *Adonai* is *a title*, also *not a name* for the <u>definitely named Creator</u> who had called Abram 'from the other side of the river' to go on the way of '<u>foreigners and sojourners</u>'; Moses from Egypt from Egypt" did *<u>revolutionise that Primordial One for his wars and conquests.</u>*

The Religious Wars

There could be no religion without miracle. Problems with the Mosaic Religion arose not from its too many miracles too much superficial for its God, but out of the fact that *that Mosaic God <u>was made anew</u>* from the very simple Hebrew *Primordial One*, *<u>was combined</u>* with the uttermost so-phisticated Egyptian *Revolutionary One*, and therefore *<u>was allowing Moses to become god-man</u>*. This very super(natural) hero did it *<u>almost all</u>*—records in the 'Holy Scriptures of the Five Books of Moses', Book II in particular.

- I appeared to Abraham, to Isaac, and to Jacob ... but my name ... was not known to them. (6:3), to Isaac, and to Jacob ... but my name ... was not known to them. (6:3)"
- I am a jealous God, visiting the iniquity of the fathers on the children to the third and fourth generations. (20:5—34:7), visiting the iniquity of the fathers on the children to the third and fourth generations. (20:5—34:7)"
- I will stretch out my hand and strike Egypt with all my wonders ... You shall plunder the Egyptians. (3:20–22)
- I will utterly blot out the remembrance of Amalek from under heaven ... generation after generation. (17:14,16)
- The Amorites and the Hittites and the Perizzites and the Cana-anites and the Hivites and the Jebusites, I will cut them off. You shall not bow down to their gods, neither serve them, nor do according to their works; but you shall utterly overthrow them and completely break down their sacred pillars. (23:23-24)
- Moses was very great in the land of Egypt, in the sight of the Pharaoh's servants, and in the sight of the Israelites. (11:3) was very great in the land of Egypt, in the sight of the Pharaoh's servants, and in the sight of the Israelites. (11:3)"
- And Moses wrote all the words of ... God ... then took the *Book of the Covenant* to read in the hearing of all the people. (24:4,6) wrote all the words of ... God ... then took the *Book of the Covenant* to read in the hearing of all the people. (24:4,6)"

Most certainly, so, were Moses able to, he would have eradicated all of the words <u>this sort</u>: *YHVH made* the earth and the skies, *YHVH formed* a human, ... then humans began to call on <u>*the name YHVH*</u>, ... *YHVH said to Abram* ... <u>*"I am YHVH who brought you out of Ur"*</u> ... . This is to point out the *Mosaic God* (be) neither as YHVH The Creator nor as the God YHVH of Abraham and Isaac and Jacod (in Canaan) and Joseph and Israel (in Egypt); and that *that Mosis from Egypt* did use The Name ***perennial*** as the very pretext for his ephemeral religious campaigns in and out of Egypt, against Pharaoh and his Egypt as well as against the Amalekites and other (six namely) peoples 'of the land'—altogether with the lot of their gods. No wonder be it, that *that god-man* 'died when his eyes were not dim nor his natural vigour abated'—in the land of Moab, at the doorstep into Canaan, not allowed to ***cross over there***.

3

The Second Moses

The next generation

The whole Mosaic generation, born in Egypt and wandering about the wildernesses those forty years, had exhaustively died out—their god-man leader included, save only Caleb and Joshua—when the appointed latter, namely *Yehshuah* in Hebraic English meaning *YHVH saves*, saves" was preparing the next generation for their 'cross over Jordan into Canaan': *A People Saved By YHVH* (Deuteronomy 33:29). This very last innovation in Mosaic style, put at the very end of Moses' *words, the final blessing on Israel*, just prior to his death as recorded by some follower of his, in concluding the last of the so-called *Five Books of Moses*, did cause too many problems for—and create too much burden upon—*his second* generation as well as endless *generations after next*, from Israelites to Jews.

The scriptural Hebrew verb for *to save*, when YHVH is the *subject*, has the particularly unique meaning: *To bestow/to pour Spirit upon the predicate*—an individual (Joshua) or a people (Israelites), not yet the *humankind* (Joel 2:28, *all flesh*) unless and until the 'Second Moses'. This is to point out the 'Israelite God' as still Mosaic after Moses as before *even though* no more Egyptian god-man ever appeared among their leaders, prophets, priests, and kings. The Spirit *abode* while a recipient remained obedient, *departed* immediately at disobedience, and *could return on conditions*—hence the 'spiritly' humans, death, and resurrection; no bodily resurrection unless and until the 'Second Moses'. Meanwhile recorded were still the jealously religious conquests *against gods of the land* together with *their peoples to be exterminated*—on coming of the <u>Ark of Covenant</u>:

- From the wilderness and Lebanon (to) as far as the Great River
- All the land of the Hittites to (as far as) the Great Sea westward

18

- Men and women, young and old, ox and sheep and donkey … utterly destroyed, their cities set on fire
- All *foreign gods*, of the other side of the River, from Egypt, and in the Land … put away, neither served nor mentioned, and in the Land … put away, neither served nor mentioned"

So, all 'the second generation born *on the way in the wilderness* circumcised *again the second time* (to become) *Sons* of Israel', that is, into the 'Lord of all the earth'—not LORD, twice at both verses 11 and 13, Joshua 3—they were most likely *not serving the Creator of the universe* but rather making *that Primordial One* serve them with their temporal desires and needs and caprices. When Achan, of the tribe of Judah, *sinned against God*, the whole religious community of the *Children of Israel* was punished, '*Israel* has sinned … *they* have become *doomed to destruction* (and) *God will not be with them ANYMORE*'—condition applies. (Joshua 7:12)

Generations after next

No condition whatsoever could be applied onto *YHVH the Creator who never changes*, either before or after Moses, who proposes the *Eternal Co-venant* at the very beginning (p. 17: *In the day human becomes like YHVH to know good and evil, human shall be surely out of Spirit*), and who did once for all state in reply to Moses, *"I will blot whoever sins against me out of my book"* (Exodus 32:33). This is to point out that YHVH will *not* be *any more / longer* with whomsoever disobedient—no bodily killings whatsoever upon Adam, Cain, and so on; neither punishment of any sorts 'to the generations third and fourth' because of the so-called 'original sin'; nor responsibility/burden upon Moses for the Israelites' sins and *vice versa*—i.e. upon the Israelites, for Achan's sin: The innovation of '*chosen people*' was Mosaic, Moses chose them to be his subjects religious for their *religious wars* whereas YHVH The Creator *called Abram and his des-cendants the Hebrews to walk on the way of foreigners and sojourners*.

The first generation after next, inside Canaan, each to one's own inheritance, <u>possessing</u> the land and *doing what was **right in one's own eyes***. This is verily the uttermost 'evil in the sight of YHVH', fore –most above all else e.g. serving the Baals and the Ashtoreths … even the near-extermination of one tribe (Benjamin) by all the others. Time and again, 'YHVH was moved to pity, rose up *judges/rulers* for them', and *saved* them but 'they turned quickly from the way': *When YHVH rose up a judge, YHVH was with the judge* all his days, but they *reverted and became more corrupt after his death*. It used to be so *generation after generation*.

The last but most revered judge/ruler, Samuel, became more renowned as *Prophet* and did himself see his own two sons he just made 'Judges over Israel' *corrupt themselves much more quickly and seriously*: They 'turned aside after dishonest gain, took bribes, and perverted justice' so much so that 'all the elders of Israel gathered together and came (back) to (Prophet) Samuel—*asking for a king to be like all the nations*. Were it the case that Israel as a whole had been *saved/chosen*, this should have been the explicit renunciation from their part: YHVH told Samuel, *"They have rejected not you but me, that I could not reign over them"*. *Fait accompli*, they by themselves confessed, "A king shall reign over us whereas *YHVH was our king*, we have added to *all our sins* the evil of asking for a king".

Saul was anointed their first king, very soon sinned against YHVH, and was rejected—not 'killed in the day', but *the Spirit departed from him* right at the moment of his disobedience to be *never returned* as he would not *repent*, instead he even sought to kill *the anointed next king*.

David was the Israelite king second but uttermost renowned for his *blood of wars* and *repentance of sins*, because of the former he might not build YHVH *a house*, but thanks to the latter he got exceedingly pardoned and famously known with this very Psalm, *"Have mercy upon me, O YHVH, according to your loving kindness. Blot out my transgression, wash me thoroughly from my iniquity, and cleanse me off my sin. For I acknowledge my transgressions, my sin is ever before me—against you, only you, have I sinned and done evil in your sight"*. Moreover King David used to get himself ready for being *punished by the hands of men*, his own sons included; so much so that he was made, from *beloved and blessed*, into *loving and blessing*—the legendary branch/source of some Davidic *Kingdom of God on earth*. This is to point out the facts that the Israelite Monarchy was founded by Saul, *not David*, according to an initiative/innovation of the Israelites, *not God's*—even *explicitly against the will of YHVH*. Israel did then overcome YHVH and, so, chances were that 'their kingdom' could not last as long as expected—actual record being to endure 'forever and ever'.

Forty years were just enough, for every out of their three kings in all, to try ruling over them and to make them become like all the nations: warring against peoples and invading other lands, then separating themselves apart and fighting one another, executing violence and bloodshed, even conducting terrorism under the banner of a religion or in the name of a god. Thousands of years later, there emerged the two 'religious empires' longest lasting ever and still warring up to this space –age—*no longer* with swords and spears that might have been *beaten into ploughshares and pruning hooks*, but actually with sorts of the so-called 'weapons of mass-destruction' that would most likely make *their flesh dissolve while they are standing on their feet, their eyes dissolve in their sockets, and their tongues dissolve in their mouths.*

For, out of the theocracy of Moses and Joshua did emerge the Israelite theocratic monarchy that began to culminate right at the enthronement of their third and last emperor, namely Solomon, of their Kingdom United that is. The 'wisest of all men ever' and among the greatest of all empire-builders, King Solomon began his days on the first by executing his brother/contender right away; liquidating the lot of opponents a bit later but not less ruthlessly, a general and even a priest included; then strengthening his position through international marital alliances of arms and trade—thereby firmly establishing his internal domination and sophisticatedly expanding his foreign reputation as well as influences, if not counting his material and territorial gains.

The Temple

*"Would you build me **a house to dwell in**? I have not dwelt in any house (but) have I ever spoken **a word to anyone**, asking 'Why have you not built me habitation of cedar?'"* YHVH thus replied King David, the most beloved and blessed but not as wise as his designated heir-son Solomon.

*"Will God indeed dwell on earth? Heaven and even the heaven of heavens cannot contain God! How much less this temple I have built! May it forever be for **The Name** that all the peoples and nations on earth should know, and that they would fear as Israel does?"* YHVH heard Solomon's prayer, sanctified his Jerusalem Temple, but solemnly warned him, 'If you or your sons at all ever turn from following me to go serving and worshiping other gods, I will cut Israel **off the land** and cast this temple **out of my sight**'.

Later on, Solomon himself and his sons and his sons' sons, almost all, did commit the sins already warned, altogether. Israel had so to be cut definitely off by the Assyrians in 722 BCE, the Temple for the Name cast ultimately out by the Babylonians in 586 BCE. Religious Scriptures and traditional teachings have it as if God were the Great Director, even the Supreme Commander, of everything aforementioned: invasion over the land, extermination against peoples thereof, and construction of the kingdom therein; then after about a century of their sins: tearing the kingdom apart, dispersing the northern Israel but sparing the southern Judah, and exiling those remnants temporarily.

In fact whenever the Israelites obeyed YHVH, they prospered; and disobeying they fell; but the other way around was not correct: They used to win and prosper *by their own*, not by God's *will*; and most if not all the other times, *they divided themselves and fell by themselves*, not by God. Seeds of the 922-BCE Secession at Shechem had been sown the century earlier at Hebron as David being made *King over Judah only*, Ben-jamin was then with *all Israel under their King.* Solomon's favouritism to his own tribe Judah was quite sensible to the northerners: As soon as his son succeeded him on the throne, they gathered themselves against *the burdens borne by our (ten) tribes*—Benjamin now came united to Judah, together they owned the Jerusalem Temple, fought the Northern Israel with its 'two alternative temples at Bethel and Dan' for two centuries, and survived the Assyrian catastrophe for over another century.

So, the Temple stood unchallenged c.960–c.922 BCE, was de-filed even in the ending of Solomon's reign by the *high places* he erected for his *foreign wives' gods*, even denied by the two *northern temples* for the worship of *golden calves* during the Secession, and destroyed in 586 BCE.

Ezra, the Scribe in Exile

The Babylonian Empire founded by Nabopolassar (626–605 BCE) de-feated and replaced the Assyrians ruling over the Ancient Near-East at the final battle of Nineveh (612), its second emperor Nebuchadnezzar (605–562 BCE) allied with the Medes of Ecbatana and succeeded whereas their predecessor had failed: Conquering Judah—597, 587–586, and 582 BCE (three deportations of Judean elites to Babylon). At the first fall of Jerusalem, Ezekiel the prophet was among the first to be exiled together with their king Jehoiachin, Zedekiah became gover-nor over Judah now a Babylonian province. During the second fall and final destruction of the Temple, because of Zedekiah's rebellion, Jeremiah was taken to some refuge along the Egyptian border—where he related the third deportation later *in the 23rd year of Nebuchadnezzar.* Meanwhile *leaders of the priests and the people,* if not killed *at the destroyed Temple* or in Riblah the land of Hamath, were taken captive to Babylon—Seraiah the high-priest included, to whom Ezra would be born most likely in exile there. Certainly no high-priest himself, Ezra sometimes was called priest-scribe or priestly scribe, but traditional Judaism revered him simply as *The Scribe*—Founder of the Great Assembly and Judaism in Diaspora, Father of the Sanhedrin and Pharisees in Judaic Tradition, even *The Second Moses* 'because if the Law had not been given to Moses, Ezra would have been its vehicle'.

Actually Ezra was the Organiser and Leader of the dispersed and exiled Judeans 'out of Judea' their homeland, in ethnic communities (in the stead of the lost Kingdom) and religious *verily new* institutions called *Synagogues* (in the stead of the lost Temple) all over the lands they were then being in—not yet the much later *World Diaspora* of the *World Jewry.* There, the *Jews* were in great need of *Scriptures*, *Torah* might not yet finalised, at least not canonised, Ezra was even 'doubtful of the correctness of some words in Torah'—some will be disregarded, others removed. Studying the Law under Baruch ben Neriah, he soon became 'a teacher well versed in Torah' and, 'with the *help* of God', be-gan <u>reconstituting</u> the Jewish life-style in Diaspora—rather than <u>rebuilding</u> the Temple 'at Jerusalem in Judea': Ezra was not among the first 'returnees from captivity' under Zerubbabel, their high-priest being Je-shua ben Jozadak. But together with his Great Assembly (of scriptural scholars) Ezra was credited with 'establishing numerous features of the Traditional Judaism' and, not so traditional, with 'restoring the Law, completing the *24-book* Scripture, and writing the 70-book *For the Wise*'.

From Synagogues to The Sanhedrin

Later from a Greek verb meaning 'to bring together', the term *synagog* meant a place of 'assembly' (house of <u>assembly</u>, *bet ha-kneset*)—private home then public/community premises primarily for worship/prayer (house of <u>prayer</u>, *bet ha-tefilla*) in lieu of the lost Temple (586 BCE) at Babylon and nearby Jewish settlements. As the Babylonian Empire de-clined speedily after the death of Nebuchadnezzar in 562 BCE, Cyrus the Persian arose seizing Ecbatana (550) and unifying the Medes into his vast and powerful Medo-Persian Empire, then definitely defeated the Babylonians (539). In the mean time, 586–539 BCE, a Diaspora of sort developed effectively into the Jewish well-organised Home-away-from-Home(-land): The system of Synagogues (at least one for every five homes) under the Great Assembly soon took *also* the charges of *bet ha-midrash* (house of <u>study</u>) and thereby, because religious study *always* implies studying Torah and practising Law and laws in Judaism, the re-ligio-judicial functions (of the later-on politico-religious *Great Sanhedrin at Jerusalem*). Ezra the Scribe did it all, from Babylonia back into Judea then outwards all over the Ancient Near-East, most likely in co-ope-ration with his followers; so much so that he has been called the *Father of Judaism* and the *Second Moses*—let alone the other traditions

- Identifying him as the Chronicler, writer of *Chronicles*
- Maintaining he *also* wrote the four non-canonical *Esdras*
- And so on with lots of *Apocalypse/Revelation, Prophecies ...,*
- Proclaiming he ended up *into heaven* like Enoch and Elijah

There are too many legends too much improbable there. Some scholars would not accept the authenticity of 'books ascribed to Esdras'. It is now established that after the 538-BCE Decree of Cyrus the Persian emperor, the first wave of Jewish returnees from the Babylonian Exile under Sheshbazzar 'Prince of Judah' could not finish the foundations of the Temple by 520 BCE: Eighteen full years of harassment, despair, and maybe 'loss of faith'. The second and major 'return of exiles' under Zerubbabel 'the governor' did accomplish rebuilding the Temple 520–515 BCE. Ezra did not *come* to the new Jerusalem Temple until 459/ 458 BCE at the earliest, not as a priest but the *Scribe of the Law of God*—this is the Persian official title granted to sort of royal secretary/com-missioner for the Jewish religious affairs, a long-time working executive of Persian administration *now commissioned to the newly established* province Judea and Temple Jerusalem, by the *fifth* Persian king (465–424 BCE).

An anointed of God

The first Persian King, Cyrus the Great (550–530 BCE), was made into an 'Anointed of God' in *Ezra, Chronicles*, and elsewhere. He had himself declared, *"I am Cyrus, King of the world; Marduk the great god rejoices at my pious acts—gathering the gods and their peoples back to their abodes at the order of the great god Marduk. May all the gods I have installed in joy to their sanctuaries, and all the peoples I have led back to their cities, (altogether) pray daily for me and the length of my life"*. From Anshan in southern Persia, of the Achaeme-nian house, Cyrus had been a Zoroastrian believing in one eternal be-neficent 'Creator' or 'Wise Lord', the *Ahura Mazda*, an honourific title for sort of wisdom-god the highest and *uniquely worthy of worship*—this is favourably enabling him to accept *Marduk* or *any other name whatsoever* for a god *made* the highest/greatest: His imperial religious policy was universalistic, tolerant, and pragmatical—radically different from both previous ones, the Assyrian uprooting deportation and the Babylonian devastating exile. No wonders, Cyrus the Great had been hailed *liberator* at his triumphant march into Babylon, 539 BCE—*half a millennium later*, he should have been (re-) named Cyrus *Christ* and titled *Lord Saviour*.

The *named* 'God of heaven', so, is likely transferred from the Babylonian *Marduk* of the 'Cyrus-cylinder' blasphemously into *Scriptures* —so much so that after eighteen full years of their arrival at Jerusalem, *the foundation of the temple was not yet laid* by those *42,360* returnees, due to their *fear of peoples in the land—adversaries of Judah and Benjamin*. A second wave of returnees under Zerubbabel came to the rescue, the founda-tion was completed in over a year of their coming to Jerusalem, 'then all the people shouted with a great shout when they praised God—*but many of the priests and Levites and heads of houses, those old men who had seen the First Temple, wept at the foundation of this temple before their eyes'*. Anyway *the temple*, from that *day of small things*, began to be built and finished *by the hands of Zerubbabel*, 520–516/515 BCE, under the third Persian King, Darius Hystaspes (522–486 BCE)—an anointed *no longer of the Babylo-nian great god named Marduk*, but of the Persian no-name universal deity *entitled Ahura Mazda*: Ezra the Scribe did not come to the (Second) Temple at Jerusalem in Judea until *the fifth month in the seventh year*, **458**, of the fifth Persian King Artaxerxes Longimanus (465–424 BCE).

How had *the situation* been looking like, there, during 516/515 – 459/458 BCE? By *the twentieth year*, **445**, *of King Artaxerxes* when Nehe-miah *the King's cup-bearer* came to the rescue, there had been **great dis-tress and reproach**—*wall broken down, gates burned with fire, city lain waste.*

Another Moses

Moses had been eighty-year old before he set up his Mosaic Religion in the wilderness. It was not recorded of the age of Ezra when he *imported* his Judaism from the Babylonian Exile *up to Jerusalem* almost sixty years after the Second Temple had been 'completed and dedicated' there, 516–458 BCE. Neither recorded was the time at which he had begun to 'prepare his heart to seek the Law, to do it, and to teach statutes and ordinances'. Let alone the year of either birth or death of so legendary such a religion-maker—Scribe, Teacher, or the like; but no Priest at all, definitely. Likely he could have been *also eighty-year old* when he *came up*:

- To inquire concerning Judah and Jerusalem *with regard to the Law* and Jerusalem *with regard to the Law"*
- To carry gold and silver the king offered *God in Jerusalem in Jerusalem"*
- To gather gold and silver and other offering from Babylon
- To buy bulls, rams, and others for the altar offerings
- To deliver articles for the service of the temple
- To set *magistrates and judges* over all peoples in the region
- To enforce the Law of God and *the law of the king* and *the law of the king"*
- To *execute judgment speedily*; be it death ... or imprisonment

No jobs exclusively to a priest among the aforementioned, but on the contrary the followings are quite exclusive to the leading maker of the strictest Mosaic monotheism: among the aforementioned, but on the contrary the followings are quite exclusive to the leading maker of the strictest Mosaic monotheism:"

- The people of Israel, the priests, and the Levites 'had to _separate themselves_ from peoples of the land'—later on the _separated ones_ would be called _Pharisees_,
- For all peoples of the land made up _abominations_ to 'the holy seed'— not only by intermarriages, but also 'with their _peace and prosperity_': The land is unclean with their uncleanness

All in all, from Zerubbabel through Ezra to Nehemiah, indigenous peoples (Samaritans) as well as aliens 'brought in by Assyrian kings' did have nothing whatsoever to do with the 'descendants of the captivity'; the so-called 'pagan wives' and their children 'born _to_ Israel' were put away _according to the counsel of **the master**_ and _according to **the law**_. Clearly enough, the put-away law relating to children born _by_ pagan wives is _not_ Mosaic, laws this sort were deduced by/originated from _the Master Ezra_ —another 'Moses' of Judaism, that is. The Master's _system of synagogues_ from Babylonia and elwhere all over the Ancient Near-East would also be imported into Judea (_bet ha-kneset_), set aside the Temple (_bet ha-tefilla_).

The third function, _bet ha-midrash_, of the system was then temporarily suspended (till the _Yeshivah_ at Jabneh in the ending of the first century CE, and the system of _yeshivot_—academies henceforth). Meanwhile, it was replaced and enhanced by the Great Sanhedrin of Jerusalem and its system of _local sanhedrim_, institutions imposed alongside those of the temple for the newly designed funtionality of _bet ha-din_, house of justice or house of judgment—ever since Ezra with certain heads of _descendants of the captivity_ were set apart and sat down to examine the matter, _questio-ning_ all the men who had taken pagan wives.

Ezra could not force the Jews anywhere within the Persian em-pire to submit unto his laws, let alone people of the land and the other peoples of the world: Religious tolerance was imperial law, policy, and practice. His ingenuity was 'tearing garment and robe, plucking hair and beard, sitting down astonished and fasting, praying and weeping' so much so that '_the people wept very bitterly and swore an oath_' to obey the 'counsel of the master', "_Yes! As you have said, so we **must** do_". And his tactics was saying 'words and counsel of his' under warranty of Moses and the Mosaic God and, as well, under protection of _that_ God's anointed— from Cyrus the king of _all the kingdoms on earth_ to Artaxerxes the king of _kings_; so much so that 'his copy of the law' with the Persian 'imperial rescript' would be extensively enforced then, authoritatively canonised later, and definitely secured 'for all time to come'.

That is, as it _had_ happened, the _Torah_ properly by the Jabneh Yeshivah in the ending of the first century CE, without _temple any longer_, neither the

Pentateuch in the *Septuagint* of a couple of centuries earlier in the Second Temple period, nor the *Tanakh* of either canons (Palesti-nian, Alexandrian) some decades later in diaspora, properly the Great Diaspora. On the other hand, the *Samaritan Torah* marked an 'ultimate terminus' of the very lengthy separation and alienation from the Jews, ever since Zerubbabel's time, both politically and religiously, through Nehemiah's determinative judgement upon those *'aliens and enemies'*, to be never reversed up until the destruction of their *Mt. Gerizim Temple* as well as their own dispersion—the Jewish ones, *destruction and dispersion*, a bit later but *equally definite*. This is to point out <u>the failures</u> of all sorts of 'housing built on earth for the One from heavens' ever since Solo-mon's, <u>*Dedicated To The Name*</u>, had been 'thrown out of sight'; and, as well, <u>the disappearance</u>, sooner or later, of all forms of 'human inven-tion, innovation, reformation, revolution, and so on' ever made out of disobedience—<u>in becoming like God to know good and evil</u>.

4

A Saviour From Sins

Jesus saved

The Hebrew for Jesus, <u>*Yeḥshuah*</u>, meant *YHVH saves* saves" , not 'Jesus saves'. The above subtitle is therefore meaning *YHVH saves Jesus*—bestowing upon him *Spirit*, maybe 'in unlimited measure'. Jesus himself had once testified, *"God is Spirit; those who worship him <u>must worship in Spirit and in Truth</u>"*. Jesus the Jew of Nazareth in the beginning of the first century CE used to call himself 'son of man'—born of humans, of flesh and blood, out of 'dust of the ground', that is. Saved by God, given of Spirit, 'born again of Spirit', he became 'son of God'.

What is Spirit? Jesus once told Nicodemus the Pharisee, a ruler of the Jews, *"The wind blows wherever it wishes, you hear its sound but cannot tell wherefrom it came and where to it is going"*. Every speculation on the Spirit is to end up nowhere. And, what is Truth? *"The Word of God is Truth"*—but which Word is it? *Everyone born of Spirit* is to hear of it.

Born again of Spirit, Jesus kept on praying for himself and for his disciples as well, the sons of God, *"O Father, I have manifested your <u>Name</u> to those you had given me out of the world ... and given them the Word you had given me. They have received and kept your word and your word is truth: Keep them <u>through your name in your word</u> that they would not be lost to evil"*. By the time Jesus was 'declaring <u>The Name</u> to the world that had not known <u>The God</u>, and preaching <u>The Word</u>', *YHVH* had been forbidden to be pronounced outside the Holy of Holies of the Second Temple for over the half-millennium, 516 BCE to 30 CE, the First dedicated to *YHVH* having already been eradicated seventy years earlier, 586 BCE. Being no high-priest, neither governor, nor scribe, Jesus got both Name and Word via Spirit; just nearly half a century after him the both began to be altered, distorted, and replaced by religious traditions via either 'rabbis and Masoretes' or 'Apostles and evangelists'.

Actually from Ezra the Scribe in Babylon onwards, the *Masoreth* (Tradition) of Judaism has got the four-letter Name 'unspeakable, never pronounced as written' whereas many a belief Persian, mostly Zoroastrian, being imported into Scriptures—5th to 4th century BCE. A millennium and a half later when the Masoretic Text of the Hebrew Scripture was finalised 'with diacritical marks, the vowel signs for correct pronunciation', it is universally authoritative to call God *Adonai* (Lord)—and to believe Word including _bodily_ *resurrection/eternality*.

On the other hand, as the Second Temple, built under Persian authority and upon Persian auspices, would soon be corrupted by the Greeks and desecrated by the Greco-Syrians, there originated the very expectation for, and prophecies on, a _Saviour from foreign domination_.

To save 'from sin'

Jesus the Jew of Nazareth came to the Hellenised Jews in Judea, then under Roman rulership (63 BCE to 475 CE), but did not save them from the Romans as having been expected to. Once they would seize him to make out a king 'by force', but he escaped to his *Father* alone: The Romans ironically crucified him (I. N.) as King of Jews (R. I.). Even his disciples also kept on insisting he should restore the kingdom.

He preached them the Sovereign Rulership of his *Father* that was 'at hand, neither here nor there, but *within you*'. Most of them heard of 'the kingdom in heaven' and did not see the Heavenly Kingship; few of them saw the Kingship but did not understand the unseen and un-seeable *King*: They began making their *at-hand Jesus* into their 'Lord and God'. Ironically, the first and foremost of all those religion-makers was of the generation next to Jesus': Saul of Tarsus 'an Israelite, of the seed of Abraham, of the tribe of Benjamin, ... having advanced in Judaism beyond many and persecuted the church beyond measure, ... neither receiving the Gospel from man nor being taught of it (by the church): It came through the revelation of ... Christ'.

In those days, the church was growing in number, of Jews and Hellenists, so much so that the Twelve Apostles summoned disciples to set up a council of seven headed by Stephen for 'the business of serving tables'; this Stephen, full of faith and power, incidently came to dispute with some of the Synagogue of Freedmen, was seized and tria-led before the high-priest (and his Great Sanhedrin in Jerusalem); at the execution of this martyr (cast out of the city and stoned to death), there was a *young man named Saul* taking care of other witnesses' clothes. Con-senting to that sentence, Saul would soon begin to 'make havoc of the church, enter every house, and drag off men and women ... to prison'.

'Still breathing threats and murder against the disciples', Saul went to the high-priest asking for permission to go on searching them in synagogues at Damascus; on the way he was caught by Christ, the said *resurrected Jesus*, made into 'the *last* to becoming *first*' out of <u>fourteen less one</u> Apostles. 'Immediately he preached the Christ, in synagogues, the Son of God *resurrected from Jesus*, ... amasing and confounding Jews'. Somehow he became 'not at all inferior to <u>the most eminent</u> of apos-tles', because, he boasted himself, *"God had separated me from my mother's womb and called me through his grace to reveal <u>his Son</u> in me, that I might preach <u>Christ among Gentiles</u>"*. That was *in the beginning of the 50s CE*, some 20 years *after the Crucifixion*: <u>*the Pauline Christ began to save humankind from sin*</u>.

A Saviour 'from sins'

'Jesus came from Nazareth of Galilee, and was baptised by John in the Jordan' according to *Mark*'s beginning of the Gospel. In *Matthew*'s, the divine progeny was added in order to make the name Jesus mean 'he will *save his people* <u>from their sins</u>'—and the man Jesus become 'God <u>with</u> us', Immanuel. Written primarily in Hebrew, *Matthew* the book began by distorting both Hebrew <u>words</u> (for virgin and Jesus, not counting the confusion between 'with' and 'in') and <u>prophecy</u> (from Isaiah). All and altogether, quite elementary if not infantile, those aforementioned were to set up a new religion more or less influenced by the born-again Saul/ Paolos/ Paulus/ Paul the Saint. This hero's writings are estab-lished to have been made public c.50 CE; the *Epistle to the Galatians* had appeared first, a decade prior to *Mark* in the 60s; after that, *Matthew* of the 70, *Luke* and *Acts* some time in the 80s when Paulus the Roman ci-tizen 'by birth' already died in home detention there—but said to have been waiting for Ceasar's final decision, 'receiving all visitors, preaching God's kingdom, and teaching Christ's things, *with all confidence as no one forbidding him*', according to *Acts*' happy ending.

The Son 'uniquely begotten' of God, in the form of God, but not self-considering equal to God, instead taking the form of no-repu-tation a servant and coming in the likeness of men, *became obedient to the point of death even on the cross*. What for? <u>Christ was offered once to bear the sins of many</u> ... *to his believers he will appear* <u>a second time for salvation</u>. It is more than enough clear: The Saviour <u>came</u> 'not to save' either from foreign oppression or from sin, but to be 'sacrificed on the cross for the sins of many' both his Jewish people and his non-Jewish believers as well. The self-same Christ <u>will come</u> back/ again, soon/ very soon/ even before '<u>this generation passes by</u>' in order to do the salvation job assigned him by Saint Paul—plus the judgement job 'over all the non-believers' as stated repeatedly in *John* and *Revelation*, ten to twenty years after Paul's *Epistles* to his churches all over the Mediterranian World.

For there is a second *In the beginning* then newly created with the Greek *Logos*, neither El nor Elohim any more: *Logos was in the beginning, with Theos, Logos was Theos*. This God 'made all things through Word', then this Word 'became flesh to dwell among us'—namely Jesus *among* Jews. An incarnated God, Jesus 'came down from heaven; from Word becoming Life, Light, Truth, Way, and so on; so much so that he could 'take away the sin of the world': Whoever believes in him should not pe-rish but have eternal life, but who does not believe is already condemned.

YHVH saves

YHVH saves 'neither by might nor by power but by his Spirit' accor-ding to Zechariah the prophet, or 'through his Name in his Word' as Jesus his Son *had* once prayed him to. YHVH did not save Adam from his disobedience, neither did he Cain from his murder, nor did he the lots of 'sons of God' from their 'great wickedness and continually evil intents and thoughts of heart'; YHVH does not change and, so, never saves any *humans whomsoever* from their sins: YHVH does save from the sin of disobedience. To become 'like God knowing good and evil' or not to become, to obey or not to obey, to sin or not to sin, that is their question: Every human without exception does have full and absolute freedom to choose, or even not to choose.

First, YHVH did nothing even to prevent Eva from choosing the fruit, Adam from eating of it, Cain from killing his brother, and so on. This is to point out there be no such thing called 'pre-destination/ pre-determinism' to be in line with the omni-scient God and in contradic-tion to the liberty of humans. Second, YHVH did not judge either Cain or Abel for the disobedience of both their parents, there is therefore no 'original sin'; on the other hand, YHVH did not kill anybody there because of his or her own sin, there is therefore no 'death sentence' bodily and hereditary—"You shall no longer use this proverb, YHVH told Ezekiel the prophet, in Israel 'the fathers have eaten sour grapes and the children's teeth are set on edge'".

Ezekiel was among the first Judean elites taken captives to Ba-bylon, 597 BCE, taking up his predecessor Jeremiah's refutation of the col-lective guilt: Every human is completely responsible to God for his/her own actions; 'Creating humans in his own image and according to his own likeness', YHVH never punishes any one, either individual or com-munity, because of the sin of anyone else—be it a parent, a leader, a king, ... even another individual or the actual generation or the previous ones ... backwards to ...

Adam. The Mosaic Religion up to the end of Solomon's Temple was also terminated, Ezekiel the prophet 'in exile' and his next-generation junior Ezra the scribe 'in exile and diaspora' did begin setting up Judaism the 'Religion of, by, and for Jews'. Let alone the legendary prophecy ascribed to 'Ezra the Scribe while in Diaspora' that the Temple in Jerusalem was to be destroyed—the very prototype of Jesus' much later; it is certainly that Zerubbabel's Temple together with Nehemiah's Wall be not from YHVH::" Cyrus the Great, worshipper of Marduk his great god; and Darius Hystaspes, of the Ahura Mazda.

The Three-Person God

Saint Paul invented Christ out of Jesus to save humankind from *sin*, half a century or so later Saint John set up a 'new beginning *antedated the Genesis-beginning*' in order that his Christ could get full authority, not on-ly to save from *sins* but also to *judge* plus to *execute* sinners (the cowardly /unbelieving /abominable /murderers /sexually immoral /sorcerers /idolaters /and all liars — in the lake which burns with fire and brims-tone) and, moreover, to *reward* the righteous and holy (in the New Jeru-salem descending out of heaven onto earth). Just a passing-by note: in singular *sin* is meaning 'against God, disobedience', *sins* are towards or relating to humans—the above three first kinds of sinners (21:8) are summed up into 'dogs' (22:15) in the ending of Saint John's *Revelation*.

Half a millennium or so later on, the Three Persons of the God –head, Roman and Catholic (from Rome to all over the Universe), would finally be defined: God the Father somewhere in the Heaven of heavens, God the Son at the right-hand side of the Father, and God the Holy Spirit—still undefined as yet, maybe undefinable because un-fathomable. A serious problem arises here: *That which is* conceived *in Mary is* of the Holy Spirit; so, this 'Third Person' should be called 'Father' of the 'Second Person', Jesus namely; then, how about the 'First Person', God The Father? Either one or both Persons *be* 'Spirit-Father of Jesus? Uttermost certainly neither one (out of the two) nor the whole three (in the one God-head) can be 'called on' by *The Name* (Hebrew): *Matthew* 1:1 uses 'Lord' three times for 'God' (only once)—there is no 'LORD' there.

Explicitly, *Mary was found with* child of the Holy Spirit (v. 18), not of her husband Joseph—let alone some Roman soldier named *Pan-thera* of a thesis on the biological father of Jesus. Any ways, Jesus was born human, 'son of man' and not 'Son of Man' in the style of *Daniel* the Book; he would much later be worshipped as a god, the Lord *Christ* rather than *Jesus*—assigned rather than anointed to the job of '*saving the whole world*': Our Lord-And-

Saviour. Much later on, by the end of the generation after next which still did not 'see' the salvation to be *'coming soon and very soon'*, *Daniel*'s Son of Man then came to the rescue: *One like the Son of Man, coming with the clouds of heaven ... to the Ancient of Days, was given dominion and glory and a kingdom that all peoples, nations, and languages* <u>shall</u> *serve him; his dominion is everlasting and his kingdom shall not be destroyed* (7:13–14). That Son of Man was revealed *'Christ on a White Horse'* with the following titles and identification: Faithful and True, The Word of God, King of kings and Lord of lords, The Alpha and The Omega, ...

To save 'from sinning'

Jesus the Jew of Nazareth has got nothing whatsoever to do with all the things religious invented decades, centuries, and millennia later. He was baptised by John the Baptist, a 'baptism of *repentance for the remission of sins*', to preach the 'gospel of the *rulership of God*'—not a 'kingdom' ei-ther here or there. The Sovereign Rulership of God is *at hand, within you*

- For from within, out of the heart of humans, proceed evil thoughts, adulteries, fornications, murders, thefts, covetous-ness, wickedness, deceit, licentiousness, evil sight, blasphemy, pride, foolishness. *All these evil things come from within and defile you;*
- For those who are well have no need of a physician, those who are sick do, I come to *call not the righteous but sinners to repentance;*
- For there is nothing hidden which will not be revealed, nor has anything been kept secret but that it should *come to light;*
- For laying aside the commandment of God, you hold *traditions* of men—washing pitcher and cup, and many other things like that; making the word of God to no effect through *traditions* you have handed down—and many such things you have done.

The above teachings *deliberately chosen* from the Gospel *according to Mark* are to expose the Jesus who came 'not to destroy either the Law or the Prophets, but to *fill them with their full meanings*'. This *deliberately taken out of context* 'quote' from *Matthew*—where the Pauline Christ had been set by a 'vergin-birth mystery' to 'fulfill' Law Mosaic/ 'that it might be ful-filled which was spoken/written by the Prophets'—is to emphasised a couple of Jesus' teachings in their very full meanings, even in *Matthew*

- You have heard that it was said to those of old, *'You shall not murder'*, whoever murders will be judged; but I tell you whoever gets *angry with his brother without a cause* shall be judged … there-fore if you bring your gift to the altar and there remember that your brother has something against you, then leave your gift there—first *be reconciled to your brother*, then come and offer gift;

- You have heard that it was said to those of old, '*You shall not commit adultery*'; but I tell you whoever *looks at a woman to lust for her* has already commited adultery with her *in his heart;*
- You have heard that it was said, '*You shall love your neighbour*' and hate your enemy; but I tell you, 'Love your enemies, bless those who curse you, do good to those who hate you, pray for those who spitefully use you and persecute you … .

"For your *Father* makes the sun rise on the evil and the good as well, and sends rain to the just as well as the unjust; if you love *only those who love you*, and greet *only your brethren*, how may you be called 'sons of YHVH'?" This is deliberately edited to be in line with the name Jesus in Hebrew—Greek, Latin, and other languages are unable to convey the very content '*I will ever be what I now am*' of the four-letter Name as well as the very meaning '*YHVH saves* saves" 'of the name *Yehshuah*.

YHVH never changes, humans always do. The Hebrews first made him the Most High—implying some Higher and High and Less High and Least High, linguistically at least; the fourth generation of theirs lost their way down to Egypt the land of bondage for dozen of generations more. Four hundred years or so later, there emerged Moses the Egypto-Israelite saving some half a million Israelites out of Egyp-tian slavery into Mosaic religious subjection—in style of Pharaoh Ak-henaton's uniquely Amarna-Age monotheism, sort of transcendental combination of cults of the triumvirate 'Re-Horakhte-Amon': Moses became sort of demi-god, 'the man–<u>god of wars</u>', and *praised YHVH* 'A God–Man of War'.

The Israelites spent some thousand years to make their history and to record it theologically: The *Hebrew scriptures* might well have been begun in part by *Moses*, but the *Canonised Scripture* did not come to light until the end of the First century CE. By then *The Name* had been infected not only by the Egyptian *Aton*, but also successively by the U-garitic *El*, the Mesopotamian *Marduk*, the Persian *Ahura Mazda*, the Greek *Zeus*, and the Roman *Jupiter*—let alone the Triune 'Father-Son-Holy Spirit' God still in the making.

Jesus came, in line with John the Baptist, urging the Jews to 're-pent'— *turning* from sin against, and back unto, the *Rulership* of utter-most likely *YHVH*, The Name Jesus was then 'making manifest'. For, '<u>through The Name and in The Word</u>' one might be '<u>saved from sinning</u>'. Un-fortunately, the Baptist was soon beheaded by a Romanised Jewish ru-ler named Herod, and a couple of years later Jesus was seized by the Jewish politico-religious authorities who accused him of rebellion against the Roman rulership: As the 'King of Jews' Jesus was cruccified according to Roman law under Pontius Pilate.

Jesus taught the way to avoid sinning against both *YHVH and humans*, did not save either himself or anyone whomsoever from any-thing whatsoever, and would not pray his *Father* to save even himself and his followers **out of this world**—let alone that world.

In lieu of an

Epilogue

'*The Sower*' parables rewritten

> *A Sower went to his field and sowed his seed of wheat;*
>
> *Some seed fell by the wayside; birds came and devoured it;*
>
> *Some fell on stony ground where it did not have much soil, It sprang up quickly but also withered away quickly—*
>
> *Being scorched by the sun and having no root deep in the ground; Some fell among thorns that grew up quicker and choked it —it yielded no crop; Other seed fell on good ground and yielded crops that increased some thirty-fold, some sixty, some a hundred.*
>
> (*Mark* 4:3–8; *Matthew* 13:3–8; Luke 8:5–8).

> *On good ground, as the seed sprouted tares also appeared.*
>
> *"Do you want us, his servants asked him, to gather up the tares?"*
>
> *"No, lest you also uproot the wheat. Let both grow together until the harvest,* **then gather the wheat first**.*"*
>
> (*After Matthew 13:24–30*)

All writers mean <u>The Word</u> by seed/grain/wheat and <u>Satan</u> 'the enemy' by birds that come quickly to take away the seed, or 'to sow the tares amidst the seed in the ground/field, i. e. hearts of men'. '<u>the enemy</u>' by birds that come quickly to take away the seed, or 'to sow the tares amidst the seed in the ground/field, i. e. hearts of men'."

Mark puts forth the parable onto human conditions and cir-cumstances: Some receive Word immediately with gladness, but having no root in

37

themselves they endure only for a time, then stumble as tribulation or persecution arises; Some also receive Word but cannot stand against the cares of this world, the deceitfulness of riches, and the desires for other things—Word becomes unfruitful; Others accept the Word and bear much fruit.

Matthew identifies the Sower as the <u>Son of Man</u> who is working in the world with his angels, against the <u>sons of the devil</u>, and for the <u>sons of the Kingdom</u> at the 'end of this age': *Then, the Son of Man will send out his angels to gather all things that offend and those who practice lawlessness—altogether shall be cast out of the Kingdom, into the furnace of fire where will be wailing and gnashing of teeth. But the righteous will shine forth as the sun in the Kingdom of their Father.*

The 'sons of the devil' should be 'first' gathered, bound, and burnt at the 'end of this age'—then the 'sons of the Kingdom' would shine: This actually is no parable (of the wheat and tares), but sort of prediction on the 'Kingdom of Heaven'—the very prototype of Saint John the Devine's *Revelation* which has got nothing <u>from</u> Jesus the Jew of Nazareth, born of Jewish parents at the 'beginning of this era'. That divine revelator would reveal *Logos* the Eternal Word a century or so after the Pauline *Christos* had already been well established.

No wonders there *be* neither *Sower of seed* nor *tares sown by the devil* there. *Christos* is *Eternal Logos* ever since a Beginning (second and last but *made into first*). Incarnated into flesh-and-blood, coming out of heavens down onto earth, that '*grain of wheat*' is to <u>die in order to produce much grain</u> (John 12:24). Christ is Sower-and-Seed at the same time all the times! Rather the parables are being combined and rewritten to point out

- the Sower: YHVH, The Creator, The Spirit, The Creator, The Spirit"
- the seed: Spirit and/or Word of YHVH and/or Word of YHVH"
- the field: humankind, the world
- the wheat: human(s) recipient(s), 'sons of God'""
- the tares: humans non-recipients, 'sons of men'
- the ground: scriptures, records, writings, ... by sons of God: scriptures, records, writings, ... by sons of God"
- birds, thorns, ... : worldly, material, ... conditions of this life.

Deliberately omitted are: Satan, enemy/enemies of God, and the likes. In the (*Genesis, First*) beginning, there are no such things—the 'serpent' being no opponent at same par to God; even later called the Dragon or Devil and named Satan *it* still is not. It might well be, however, the very 'Adversary of

Christ' in style of the Persian *Ahriman* vs *Ohrmazd*, spirit-sons of the *Ahura Mazda*.

This Persian *wisdom-god* is highest, uniquely to be worshipped over all spirits, immortals, daevas, ... according to the so-called Persian 'dualist monotheism' or Zoroastrianism—after its priest and founder Zoroaster (Zarathustra), c. 628–551 BCE, the very making period of the Hebrew scriptures; some striking similarities that can be found are

- Creator of both material and spiritual worlds, of both material and spiritual worlds,"
- Sovereign lawgiver, originator of morality, judge of all worlds,
- Holy spirit, spirit of truth, spirit of righteousness, ...
- Kingdom of truth, justice, bliss, immortality, ... of truth, justice, bliss, immortality, ..."
- Kingdom of lie, evil, condemnation, ... of lie, evil, condemnation, ..."
- Freedom of choice/decision, but *no reversal possible.*

Latent in the Hebrew, the following are manifested in the Greek *Bibles*

- Final judgment, existence after death, bridge of requiter,
- Everlasting life-in-light and horror-in-darkness,
- Renewal of worlds, resurrection of the dead. of the dead."

This is to point out merely some of the *'tares'* that have been sprouting from *'the ground'* for a couple of millennia, even up to *2008—The pro-phesied end-time reveals* the demise of the US *and the beginning of* man's final war.' for a couple of millennia, even up to *2008—The pro-phesied end-time reveals* the demise of the US *and the beginning of* man's final war."

A final witness, an end-time prophet, 'of the God of Abraham', wrote, "By the fall of *2008*, the United States will have collapsed as world po-wer, or it will have begun its collapse and no longer exist as indepen-dent nation within six months after that time"—Today: 08 Jan. 2010.

"In the past 1900 years, have you ever read or heard of a publication from any religious leader who has made such claims, laying out such a precise pattern for the near future with such precise timelines? You have not! This is the evidence (witness, testimony) of the true God of Abraham".—But I do have, Dear Reverend.

What do I think I am?

I do not think, I know and am definitely sure: I am nothing but dust. This has been so ever since I turned forty-seven, 'in three days I was destroyed'— eradicated of all and altogether the things of the previous 'fourty-six-year' edification. Early morning the fourth, of that Easter season, I had been checked up for the last time to see whether or not I did 'still' believe I am made of 'dust taken out of the ground' before the Pastor ministering that Vietnamese Evangelical Church baptised me Christian. "Definitely, Reverend!"—and the Pastor reluctantly did his religious job, telling me after the ceremony, "Never before had I ever known anyone 'believe' thanks to a single verse of the Old Testa-ment. Be sure and remember, 'We are no religion, but the way of life; we cannot teach a professor of philosophy our religion if any; let us pray the Holy Spirit for our way of life'."

It was then so peculiar a way of existence, indeed. Not a human life at all, a bestial struggle for life at best, even worse than a hunted beast, I had to be always moving all around. I am afraid no languages can ever express my existing experiences there. Any ways I had to live '*not by food alone, but also by the Word*'—arduously and all the time studying the Holy Bible. I could not recall exactly, so I would not retell here the tale of, how I have survived those miserable years inside that red paradise, sort of self-exile at own birth-place, since that mise-rable year until the day I was literally taken out of that miserable coun-try—accurately four years after I had been saved '*neither by might nor by power but by The Spirit*'. On grounds of theses latter four I do firmly be-lieve in The One who '*feeds birds of the air and clothes lilies of the field*', and of those former eleven I am absolutely sure my Saviour *makes the sun rise on the evil and the good as well, and sends rain to the just as well as the unjust* —giving me a name as mine at birth being completely erased long ago.

What do I think I do?

Born non-English speaking I had studied things in French and English, having so never thought of writing anything whatsoever in this third language—till the day I was planted in Adelaide southern Australia. I was then too old to get a job and make a living on my own, having two decades before used to be living on sort of 'bread and meat brought by the ravens, and water sprang out of the brook there'.

Neither religions nor theologies ever were the subjects of my studies; instead it had been mathematics and physics, philosophy and pedagogy. Therefore I had to leave the Bible College of South Australia after only one term there—within my first year here, sort of 'land of re-guge'. Previously there had been an 'island of refuge', the Indonesian 'Galang Refugee Camp', wherein I was kept three and a half years for the UNHCR's Screening—actually for my first-time-ever hearing of an accusation, bold and public and authoritative because official, on Chris-tianity: Both Jews and Christians are unfaithful, though believers and peoples of the Book—they have distorted even their own scriptures.

'Better have no books than believe only one' I used to seriously study every of all the books that happened to fall into my hands or run onto myself—I mean both written whatsoever and living whomsoever ones. Anyway, for the whole second half of my life now *beyond the tombs* of mine *there*, I have got nothing at all to do but studying such books of which no bibliography could ever be available—all the while awaiting for the uttermost sure 'return as dust to the ground'.

By 'studying books', the holy 22 or 24, 39 or 46, and counting, and else not so holy, I mean 'first gather the wheat' as much the thirty-fold, sixty, a hundred ... or as possible—regardless of 'the tares' that might well be offended, tramped, and even uprooted. This is to point out '*The Word that goes forth from YHVH*': *It shall not return void but shall accomplish that for which it is sent ... For, instead of the thorn shall come up the cypress tree, and instead of the brier the myrtle tree; It shall be to YHVH for a name, an everlasting sign never to be cut off.*

In those not-so-good old days, when a servant would not deli-ver a Word, YHVH made a very stubborn mule or the hardest rock speaking; instead of either an obedient speck of dust is nowadays to be writing out the primordial, unique, and simplest Covenant: Human cre-atures always are absolutely free to choose whether or not becoming like YHVH The Creator *to know/define/determine* good and evil. Abraham and the Hebrews up to Joseph chose ***not to*** on their ***way of sojourners***.

But Moses and his Israelite subjects, as well as part of their descendants even up until nowadays, did choose to—taking laws and the Law into their own hands on their way of conquerors. Seed of 'tares' had been sowed, roots of 'all evil' have been grown, and 'large branches' of powers dividing then conflicting against one another are shadowing all over present-day world and humankind. So much so that postmodern prophets of all sorts are confidently predicting some 'final' war.

Actually there are two canonised versions of <u>the final war</u> and uncountable unauthorised ones of the second. The first was prophesied repeatedly by the Hebrew last prophets, making God fight against 'the proud who did wickedly', burn them up like in an oven, and leave them '<u>neither root nor branch</u>' ... 'their flesh shall <u>dissolve</u> while they stand on their feet, their eyes in their sockets and their tongues in their mouths'. The second was revealed by Saint John the Divine: Christ sat on a white horse, clothed with a robe dipped in blood, and 'struck the nations with a sharp sword out of his mouth...'—both versions most likely are of the self-same war because Saint John made God incarnated into Christ, 'King of kings and Lord of lords, Beginning and End, First and Last ...'. Other versions have been set up by 'witnesses', sometimes also called 'prophets', relating to a <u>Second Coming of the 'Son of Man'</u> —previously created by an anonymous writer of *Danel* the Book, a wri-ting about *Danel* a personality of old, <u>the name Daniel being of no pro-phets in the Hebrew Scripture</u>.

This is to point out some things I never do, neither believe, nor think I could either do or believe: Future telling, Vision creating, Religion making, and the likes. The 'fall of 2008' happened to fall upon the sixtieth anniversary of the State of Israel: In line with the long-standing tradition of <u>Time setting</u>, the aforementioned 'end-time prophet' foretold *the demise of the United States*, that is, the collapse of Israel—verily the prelude to an *end-time war*, thus setting *World War III within six months* after that. As I have been studying the Hebrew Scripture for the past twenty-four years, I am certain that a prophet is called by YHVH for delivering some Word or Message of his, never for predicting any future far or near of humans. In this very sense, I am also verily certain <u>I am no prophet at all</u>—but merely a human, made of dust, saved by YHVH, enabled to study The Word of *his* and to get *my* studies published for the sake of <u>people like me</u>, as well as of <u>peoples like mine</u>, <u>the uprooted and displaced and dispersed to all over the world 'on the way of sojourners'</u>, *never ever receiving any* <u>revelations</u> *on either Word or Message*.

As the wind blowing blowing"

Once upon a time, I had been like a bat that birds would not recognise as of their species—neither could rats as of theirs... Three times I was dead and entombed... however I definitely chose, was and am happy with, that situation—in order to try living up my people's legacy, to no avail actually because generations of ours had already been wasted away

On the other hand, I have also been quite happy, I thought, I could have comprehended how come that 'four out of five Children of Israel presently are still in their Diaspora'—well over half a century after the State of Israel had been established.

Lest further and furthermore generations be lost... efforts of no avail are to be made. Unfortunately, no longer am I of my people—and never of the Jewish's, spiritually, that is. Meanwhile, there could be no way for one to be checked whether he or she belongs to this or that people, biologically.

So, in regards of all the 'into-Diaspora dispersed', without any discrimination, I wished we would breathe in and taste up The Free Wind wherever we have gone to—on our way of sojourners and regardless whomsoever we had been of.

For, thus said YHVH the Creator, *"With mercies I will gather you unto me, and with kindness I will show upon you my everlasting love"*—provided that we do will, otherwise YHVH the Spirit could do nothing for us and does have nothing to do with us.

Excerpts from:

*As the wind blowing **blowing"***
August 2005, 0-595-36888-3
(pp. 1–2; 31–32)

Beyond The Tombs
September 2005, 0-595-37144-2
(pp. 219–220; 247-248)

Published by iUniverse, Inc., USA

43